Action
Research
for Kids

Preface

Thank you for selecting this book! We hope you enjoy exploring the units presented. This collection of lessons allows students to participate in changing their schools, communities, and lives based on the findings of their research. Implicit in action research is *action*. We challenge you and your students to be active change agents within your community through the suggestions provided in the two action lessons included in each unit. When students "own" their educational journeys, they are more invested in learning and motivated by the learning process. The excitement and passion these lessons have the potential to elicit from students is unbounded. Have fun with the learning process and encourage your students to do the same.

Because a book of this nature has not existed before, we are interested in receiving your compliments, critiques, suggestions, and any other forms of feedback you are compelled to provide. We hope to build on this initial base to create publications similar to this one, but broader in scope, content, and audience. Your input is essential as we go forward. Please correspond with author Amanda Latz via e-mail; she can be reached at amandaolatz@gmail.com. Feel free to send text, photos, and other media.

Thank you once again!

Introduction to the Units

We envision this book as a practical guide for educators interested in using critical differentiation (Latz & Adams, 2011). Five action research units for high-ability learners in the upper elementary and lower middle school grades are presented. Two units take a quantitative approach (survey and experimental research) and three units take a qualitative approach (life history, photovoice, and playbuilding). Each unit is composed of six lessons: one preteaching lesson for scaffolding, three regular lessons to introduce the concepts, and two action lessons to effect change.

Most lessons consist of three parts: Preparation, Implementation, and Differentiation. Preparation includes the following sections: Purpose, Students Will Know, Students Will Understand, Students Will Be Able To, and Materials Needed. It also includes a Resources section when applicable. Implementation includes a step-by-step outline of how to execute the lesson. These two parts can be found in all lessons. The Differentiation section includes specific information on how to differentiate each lesson to meet the needs of students with varying levels of ability.

Units can be implemented in any order. Four preparatory lessons are included at the start of the book to provide students with an overview of the overarching theme of this book: action research. Implementing the units out of order may require an implementation of the four preparatory lessons first.

For all lessons in this book, the following Common Core State Standards in English Language Arts are addressed:

- Text Types & Purposes,
- Research to Build and Present Knowledge, and
- Range of Writing.

In addition, Units 1 and 2 (Section 3: Quantitative Research) address the following Common Core State Standards in Mathematics:

- Measurement & Data
- Statistics & Probability, and
- all Mathematical Practices.

Given the current standards-driven educational culture, connecting lessons with specific standards is critical. The inclusion of this information provides a means of justifying lessons to administrators, parents, and other stakeholders.

Theoretical Background

Critical differentiation (Latz & Adams, 2011) is a merger of critical pedagogy and differentiation. This concept was created as we looked outside of the literature on gifted education to attempt to address the unique needs of students who are both gifted and of poverty. We have termed children of poverty with gifts and talents as *twice oppressed*. In sum, critical differentiation is a means to understand and unravel the unique situation of the twice-oppressed child. Most importantly, it is a way to reach twice-oppressed children, and all children, pedagogically.

Rationale for Lesson Plan Outlines

As stated previously, most lessons consist of three parts: Preparation, Implementation, and Differentiation.

The Preparation section provides the educator with a guide for planning the lesson. The following information is included in the Preparation section:

- **Purpose**—What is the purpose of this lesson? What are the essential understandings? What key concepts are involved?
- **Students Will Know**—A list of vocabulary words, with definitions, pertaining to the lesson. This is included for most lessons (some lessons do not introduce new vocabulary).
- **Students Will Understand**—A summation of what students are expected to learn in this lesson.
- **Students Will Be Able To**—A list of skills and activities students are expected to perform and complete.
- **Materials Needed**—If any materials are needed for the lesson, they are listed. Any worksheets, handouts, and rubrics needed are included here as well.

- **Resources**—Additional readings, websites, films, or other pertinent resources are provided for some lessons. This section is not included in all lessons.

The Implementation section includes step-by-step, easy to follow instructions for executing the lesson. Teachers are encouraged to modify the lessons to meet the needs of their schools, classrooms, or student groups. For example, Unit 1's Action Lesson 1 provides the example of oatmeal raisin cookies versus chocolate chip cookies. These two types of cookies can be substituted for any number of items offered, or not offered, by the school's cafeteria. Each lesson includes a variety of assessments, activities, and/or rubrics, the use of which are explained in this section. These handouts, worksheets, and rubrics can be found at the end of each lesson.

The Differentiation section provides ideas regarding how to modify the lessons to meet the needs of diverse learners within a single classroom or student group. Students inevitably vary in terms of ability, readiness, and culture. To reach all students educationally, their individual needs must be taken into consideration. This section reduces guesswork and allows teachers to match students' skills with the appropriate challenge. This section is included for most, but not all, lessons.

Differentiating the Lessons

Use of the preassessments, where applicable, can assist in decision making about differentiation strategies and grouping for students. Each lesson can and should be modified with the students in mind. Careful consideration must be given to the students' attributes as well as the educational context within which learning will take place. The Differentiation sections offer specific ways in which content, process, and products can be differentiated.

Section 2
Introduction to Research

Preparatory Unit

These lessons are designed to teach students about research in a broad sense. They are also designed to prepare students for the forthcoming action units.

What You Will Find in This Unit

PREPARATORY LESSON 1

What Is Research?

Preparation

Purpose: To understand the broad concept of research.

Students Will Know:
- **Application** (noun): A way in which something is used.
- **Hypothesis** (noun): A proposed explanation.
- **Knowledge** (noun): A collection of information that is known.
- **Research** (noun or verb): A systematic study of a topic that yields new, confirms previous, or counters previous knowledge, theories, or applications.
- **Researcher** (noun): An individual who engages in research.
- **Scientific method** (noun): The process for experimentation; a way to empirically address a research question (for more information, see Handout 1).
- **Systematic** (adjective): Anything that involves a plan, method, or system.
- **Theory** (noun): A proposed explanation of a phenomenon.

Students Will Understand:
- the broad concept of research.

Students Will Be Able To:
- explain the scientific method, and
- articulate and create a feasible research action plan.

Instructional Strategies Used:
- Whole-group instruction
- Think-pair-share

Materials Needed:
- Copies of Preassessment
- Preassessment Rubric
- Copies or visual display of The Scientific Method handout
- Copies or visual display of Research Topic Narrowing Example handout
- Paper for students to take notes/brainstorm

- Copies of Postassessment
- Postassessment Rubric
- Copies of What Is Research? Choice Board handout

Implementation

Time Needed:
- *Part 1:* 25 minutes
- *Part 2:* 45 minutes
- *Part 3:* 25 minutes

Instructions:

Part 1
- Explain to students that they will soon be starting a unit on one of the five areas of action research presented in this book. Before doing so, it is important that the students have a solid base of understanding and knowledge about research as a broad concept.
- Explain to the students that it is important for you to learn about each student's prior knowledge on the broad topic of research so that you will know in which direction to take the lesson. Encourage students to do their best work. Emphasize that the preassessment is *not* taken for a grade.
- Provide each student with the preassessment sheet. Allow students approximately 20 minutes to complete it. You can ask students to type or write their responses.
- Collect the preassessments. Score the preassessments using the Preassessment Rubric. Retain the results for use in establishing learning scaffolds and grouping.

Part 2
- Explain to students that research is a way for individuals to better understand the world. Research can add to what is already known about a certain topic. Just about any topic they can think of can be researched.
- Provide students with a brief explanation of the scientific method. Explain that the scientific method provides a systematic way of exploring a research topic or question. Use The Scientific Method handout in any way you see fit. Emphasize that the process is typically circular, rather than a series of linear steps. The researcher enters at different points and can sometimes skip steps, repeat steps, or move through the steps out of order. Research can sometimes be messy.

- Ask students to recall the topics on which they wanted to do research; they listed these on the preassessment. First, ask students to think about how they would narrow the scope of their topics. Explain the importance of having a focused topic. A research topic that is too broad will become cumbersome and difficult to manage. Use the Research Topic Narrowing Example handout, or create your own relevant to the students' lives or based on a topic you are exploring in another discipline. Ask for an example from a student and work through the narrowing process as a whole group. Create the concentric circles so that all students can see the graphic develop (either with an overhead, LCD projector, SMART Board, or a white board).

- Explain how the narrowed research topic ought to be converted into a research question in order to go forward with the research. Based on the example provided in the Research Topic Narrowing Example handout, a possible research question is: Do both pumpkin and green bean seedlings grow toward the sun? Ask students to consider other ways to frame a research question on this topic. What is the relationship between the hypothesis and the research question? Explain to students that oftentimes more than one research question guides the research process. Ask the students if they can think of more than one research question related to the seedlings. Discuss the research questions students offer as a whole class.

- Think-pair-share: Ask the students to brainstorm ways to carry out research that would allow them to answer or address the research question above. Ask them to write out their ideas in any way they see fit using words and drawings. Suggest they use free writing, an outline, a concept map, or recreate a circular figure similar to that used on The Scientific Method handout using their own ideas specific to this research question. After a few minutes of brainstorming, ask students to pair up and compare their ideas. When facilitating the grouping, consider the students' preassessment scores. Next, ask the student pairs to merge into groups of four or six and compare ideas across pairs. Finally, discuss the ideas as a whole class. Ask students to evaluate their ideas against the scientific method. Ask students if their research plan would allow them to address or answer the research question. Is it systematic? How can it be improved?

- Conclude the lesson with a series of questions for the students to consider. Ask them to imagine their research plan has been carried out. Based on the potential results, what new knowledge could be generated? How could theories be generated from the results? How could the research results be applied to the real world? What might the potential results mean?

Part 3
- Provide each student with the postassessment sheet and allow them approximately 20 minutes to complete it.
- Explain to students that you would like to know what they learned during the lesson on research. Each of the action research units requires some foundational knowledge about research as a broad and general concept.
- Emphasize that the postassessment is not taken for a grade. It is simply a way for you to understand more about what students learned through the implementation of the lesson.

Differentiation

- Provide each student with the What Is Research? Choice Board, which is based on the example research question regarding bean and pumpkin seedling growth used in the lesson.
- Ask each student to complete three of the choices on the board using the concept of tic-tac-toe. Students must choose a "winning" combination: three options in a row going across, up or down, or diagonally.
- Either collect students' work, ask them to present their work to the class or in small groups, or ask them to complete the work as an anchoring activity.
- Students' work can be used simply as an activity or for a grade.

WHAT IS RESEARCH?

Preassessment

1. Write a paragraph on any topic and include the following four words: *research, systematic, hypothesis,* and *application.*

2. List five topics on which you would like to do research.

3. Select one of the five topics you listed above and describe how you would conduct your research.

WHAT IS RESEARCH?

Preassessment Rubric

	5	4	3	2	1	0	Points Earned
Question 1	All four words were used properly within the context of a logical paragraph.	Three words were used properly within the context of a logical paragraph.	Two words were used properly within the context of a logical paragraph.	One word was used properly within the context of a logical paragraph.	No words were used properly within the context of a logical paragraph.	No words were used. A logical paragraph was not provided.	
Question 2	Five topics were listed.	Four topics were listed.	Three topics were listed.	Two topics were listed.	One topic was listed.	No topics were listed.	
Question 3	Five or more research steps were provided.	Four research steps were provided.	Three research steps were provided.	Two research steps were provided.	One research step was provided.	No research steps were provided.	

Comments:

Total Points Earned: _____/(15)

THE SCIENTIFIC METHOD

Decide on a topic, develop a research question

Conduct background investigation

Create a hyphothesis

Conduct an experiment

Analyze data and report results

Evaluate hypothesis

RESEARCH TOPIC
NARROWING EXAMPLE

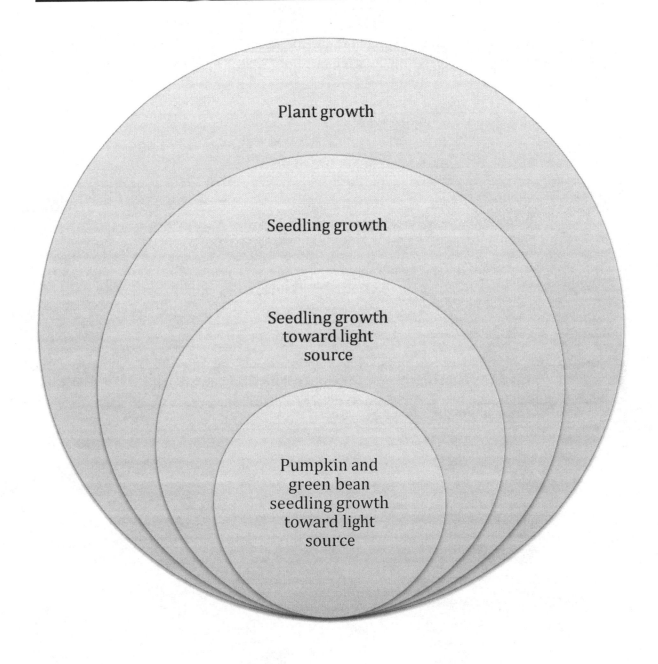

Plant growth

Seedling growth

Seedling growth
toward light
source

Pumpkin and
green bean
seedling growth
toward light
source

Name:_____Date: _____

WHAT IS RESEARCH?

Postassessment

1. Think back to the five topics on which you would like to do research. Select one and turn that research topic into a narrow research question. Write your research question below.

2. Create a plan for conducting your research based on the question above. Write out your research plan below. You can use a mix of words and drawings.

WHAT IS RESEARCH?

Postassessment Rubric

	5	4	3	2	1	0	Points Earned
Question 1	N/A	N/A	A logical and narrow research question was provided.	A logical research question was provided, but it was too broad.	A research question was provided, but it was not logical or narrow.	No question was provided.	
Question 2	A well-articulated research plan was provided. The plan was comprehensive and organized in a sensible and meaningful way.	A well-articulated research plan was provided. The plan was somewhat comprehensive and organized in a sensible and meaningful way.	A research plan was provided. The plan was somewhat comprehensive and organized in a sensible and meaningful way.	A research plan was provided. The plan was somewhat comprehensive, but not organized in a sensible or meaningful way.	A partial research plan was provided, but it was not organized in a sensible or meaningful way.	No research plan was provided.	
						Total Points Earned: _____	/(8)

Comments:

Name:_____ Date: _____

WHAT IS RESEARCH? CHOICE BOARD

Conduct a web scavenger hunt on the term *phototropism*. Create a concept map on a large piece of paper using words and images that expresses what you found, or use MindMeister (http://www.mindmeister.com) to create the concept map.	Search online for at least three examples of experiments on the topic of phototropism. Select one that you would like to replicate. Then, create a detailed budget outlining all costs associated with the experiment. You can use paper or spreadsheet software.	A friend of yours has a houseplant that keeps falling over! Your friend says that the plant has grown heavily to one side of the pot and is unstable. Brainstorm five questions to ask your friend about the situation so that you can help him or her fix the problem. Imagine that it is determined that the plant is growing toward the only available light source. Brainstorm two detailed plans you could suggest to your friend to solve the problem.
Create five research questions based on the research topic discussed in class. Then, create at least two possible hypotheses for each question. Finally, among the hypotheses for each question, decide which one you think is correct. Explain why.	Conduct a web scavenger hunt on the phrase *Three Sisters Garden*. Present your findings as a PowerPoint or Prezi presentation (http://www.prezi.com). Include an explanation of how this phrase might be connected to the research question explored in class.	You have decided that you would like to become a researcher when you grow up. Think of three people you are familiar with who might be able to provide you with some advice on this career plan. Imagine that you are planning to interview each of the three people. Create a set of five questions for each of your three interviewees. Make sure each set of questions is unique. Be prepared to explain why you selected the people you chose.
Explore this website: http://www.schoelles.com/Science/sciphototropism.htm. Compose an executive summary of the experiment and include why this research is important.	Imagine that you are designing a greenhouse. Considering what new knowledge may be generated by the research plan discussed in class, how would you construct the greenhouse? Use materials supplied in class to create a model greenhouse. Use the Internet as a resource. Be prepared to explain your design rationale.	You are going to carry out research based on one of the seedling questions posed in class during the lesson on the scientific method. You have decided to keep a researcher's journal. Be prepared to discuss why you would make that decision and what your journal would contain. Create two detailed sample hypothetical entries for your journal.

PREPARATORY LESSON 2

What Is the Difference Between Quantitative and Qualitative Research?

Preparation

Purpose: To understand the difference between quantitative and qualitative research.

Students Will Know:

- **Qualitative research** (noun): "An approach to social science research that emphasizes collecting descriptive data in natural settings, uses inductive thinking, and emphasizes understanding the [participant's] point of view" (Bogdan & Biklen, 2007, p. 274).
- **Fieldwork** (noun): Work done in the field of research such as exploration, observations, and interviews.
- **Interview** (noun and verb): A meeting in which one or more individuals ask questions of and/or converse with another person or persons about a topic (noun); to have a meeting with another individual to ask questions or converse about a topic (verb).
- **Observation** (noun): An act of instance or watching, perceiving, and/or noticing attentively.
- **Ethnography** (noun): A branch of anthropology that consists of the systematic description of individual cultures; a written product consisting of a systematic description of an individual culture.
- **Culture** (noun): A group of individuals who all share the same or similar ways of living with regard to values, behaviors, language, dress, food, symbols, and so forth.
- **Interpret** (verb): To provide meaning.
- **Quantitative research** (noun): An approach to social science research that emphasizes systematically investigating a topic, such as a social phenomenon, via statistical or computational techniques.
- **Generalize** (verb): To form general principles or opinions; to infer that the results from one group or sample involved in a research study apply to other, similar groups or samples.

- **Researcher bias** (noun): A particular tendency or inclination had by an individual conducting research.
- **Population** (noun): A large and defined group of individuals from which a smaller group of individuals is recruited or selected to participate in a research study.
- **Sample** (noun): A group of individuals involved in a research study.
- **Control group** (noun): A collection of individuals involved in a research study that is not exposed to treatment and to which the experimental group is compared.
- **Experimental group** (noun): A collection of individuals in a research study that is exposed to treatment and to which the control group is compared
- **Variable** (noun): A changeable feature or factor such as age or weight.
- **Data** (noun): Items of information. (*Note*: data is plural; datum is singular.)
- **Predict** (verb): To assert in advance.
- **Reliability** (noun): The degree to which an instrument yields the same results during repeated trials.
- **Validity** (noun): The degree to which an instrument measures what it is meant to measure.
- **Statistics** (noun): Numerical facts or data themselves.
- **Replicate** (verb): To repeat.
- **Cause** (noun): A reason or motive.
- **Effect** (noun): Something produced by a cause; consequence.
- **Correlation** (noun): A mutual relation of two or more things.
- **Analysis** (noun): A study of the nature of something and the determination of its elemental parts and their relationships to one another.

Students Will Understand:
- the difference between quantitative and qualitative research.

Students Will Be Able To:
- differentiate between quantitative and qualitative research.

Instructional Strategies Used:
- Guided inquiry
- Small-group work
- Case study
- Games
- Web-based inquiry
- Exit cards

Materials Needed:
- Copies of Research Scenarios 1–5
- Highlighters (one per student)
- Copies of Research Words handout
- I Have/Who Has? Cards
- Copies of Exit Card handout

Implementation

Time Needed: 45 minutes (all parts)

Instructions:

Part 1
- Start the lesson by asking the students to think about different ways in which research might be conducted. Ask students to voice some of the ideas they have.
- Tell the students to keep these ideas in mind. Then, ask students if they can describe the difference between *quantity* and *quality*. Once the difference has been determined, ask them if they can determine the difference between the words *quantitative* and *qualitative*. Ask the students what these two words might have to do with research.
- Explain to the students that research is conducted within one of two major methodological umbrellas, quantitative and qualitative, and that sometimes research projects involve methods from both research paradigms, which is called mixed methods research. Provide a brief explanation of the difference between the two major approaches.
- Distribute a highlighter and a copy of the research scenarios to each student. Have the students read each scenario and determine if the research methodology described is quantitative or qualitative research. After students have the determination, ask them to highlight the words within the scenario that prompted them to choose quantitative or qualitative research. Once the students have finished, go over their responses as a whole group.
- Tell students that if they finish before their classmates they should begin to compose their own research scenario. Distribute the Research Words handout to these students. Their scenarios should be at least one full paragraph and fall squarely within one of the two research paradigms. Once their paragraphs are completed, they can swap with a classmate and repeat the process of determining whether the scenario represents quantitative or qualitative research and highlighting clue words.

Part 2

- Provide the whole class with the Research Words handout.
- Ask the students to each create one study tool for learning the words. Below is a chart that represents some potential ways students can create study tools based on learning styles in a general sense. Allow the students to chose their own means or guide them based on their styles.

Visual	Auditory	Kinesthetic
Word Find	Audio Recording of Words and Definitions	Flash Cards With 3" x 5" Cards (and Clothespins— Optional)
Crossword Puzzle	Video Recording of Words and Definitions	Cubes
PowerPoint Slides	Compose a Rap or Jingle Containing the Research Words	Board Game

- Break the students up into groups based on category or preferred learning style. Ask them to swap and try one another's study tools.

Part 3

- Once the students have completed, swapped, and tried each other's study tools, pass out the I Have/Who Has? Cards. There are a total of 25 cards. If you have less than 25 students in your class, you can give students more than one card.
- Play one round of I Have/Who Has? The student who has the START and FINISH card begins the game.
- Mix up the cards and play another round or two.
- At the close of the session, pass out the Exit Card to the students. You will use this as a form of assessment. Ask students to complete the card and pass it back to you.

Differentiation

- Ask students to complete a web scavenger hunt based on their responses to the second prompt on the Exit Card.
- Ask students to create a wiki or social bookmarking webpage based on what they compile from the scavenger hunt.

- Ask students to work independently and then arrange their work in a way that other students (within the class or in future classes) can view and use.
- This activity can be used as an anchoring activity. Students' work can be used simply as an activity or for a grade.

RESEARCH SCENARIO 1

Members of Blue Whale Elementary School's Student Government Association (SGA) are interested in creating five student organizations to promote the development of friendship, leadership, and engagement among and within students of all grades. To create student organizations, the SGA must find a way to know what types of organizations match students' interests. The SGA decided to create an online survey to send to each student. The survey included a list of 20 possible student organizations, and students were to select an unlimited number of organizations in which they were interested from the group of 20. There were 318 surveys returned from the 545 students enrolled at Blue Whale Elementary School. This indicated a response rate of 58%. Among the 318 students who returned surveys, the top five potential organizations were:

- Students With Pets (34%),
- Graphic Novel Club (22%),
- Students for the Protection of the Environment (21%),
- Student Volunteers (19%), and
- School Beautification Team (19%).

Using these data, the SGA members were able to present their ideas to school officials and receive funding for each organization. In addition, many teachers were eager to serve as advisors for the newly formed student groups.

RESEARCH SCENARIO 2

Ms. Clark is the head coach of the school's track team. At the beginning of each season, she requires each of her long-distance runners to complete a timed mile, or four laps around the track. This is the very first thing she asks of the runners. All of the runners' mile times are recorded in a spreadsheet. Ms. Clark also asks her runners to complete another timed mile at the very end of the season. These times are also saved in the database. For the past two track seasons, the runners have dropped their mile times by an average of 54 seconds from the start to the finish of each season: 52 seconds two years ago and 56 seconds one year ago. Ms. Clark has used the same training schedule for her long-distance runners for the past 2 years, but she would like to try some new techniques this season. The new techniques include one day of weight training per week and 2 days of guided stretching per week. At the end of this year's track season, the average mile time decreased by an average of 67 seconds. Ms. Clark was very pleased with the results of the new training schedule and plans to continue to experiment with new ways of increasing the speed of her long-distance runners.

RESEARCH SCENARIO 3

The orchestra at Lower Nestle County Middle School, which serves fifth through eighth grade students, has adopted a peer-mentoring program to help young musicians make the shift from elementary to middle school orchestra. The program has been a huge success! Mr. Bishop, the current orchestra director who started the mentoring program 7 years ago, is interested in sharing the program with the newly hired band director, Mr. Huffle. However, Mr. Bishop is interested in better understanding the student mentor and mentees' perspectives on the program. Most of the program's positive feedback has come from informal notes, e-mail messages, and comments from parents or guardians of students involved. Fifth-grade student mentees are paired with seventh-grade student mentors when they arrive to middle school orchestra practice on the second day of school. The mentorship lasts for 1½ years. When orchestra students are halfway through their sixth-grade year, they begin to prepare to mentor the following year's fifth graders. When orchestra students are halfway through their eighth-grade year, they begin to prepare for high school orchestra by attending performances and practicing with the high school orchestra once per week. Mr. Bishop plans to interview four mentor-mentee pairs during the month of October. He wants to understand what they think of the program and how it works. He plans to conduct each of the eight interviews separately. Once the interviews are conducted, he will analyze the information, prepare a report, and share the report with Mr. Huffle. Mr. Huffle will then use the report to help him create a similar program for the band.

RESEARCH SCENARIO 4

Ms. Hutchings teaches a variety of classes within the culinary arts at Waterville Elementary School. She is interested in learning more about students' interests in cooking and baking. In addition, she is interested in better understanding what parts of her classes her former students enjoyed the best in terms of their learning. To do this, she decides to invite her former students from last year's classes to attend one of three focus groups. Each focus group will consist of five to eight students. During the focus groups, Ms. Hutchings will prepare a number of new dishes and pastries for the students to sample. These new items may become a part of subsequent classes. Ms. Hutchings will consider the students' feedback with regards to these items. She has prepared a list of questions to ask the students regarding what they enjoyed about their culinary arts classes:

- Which dish or pastry did you enjoy preparing the most?
- Which dish or pastry was the most difficult to prepare?
- Did you enjoy the video clips we viewed? Why or why not?
- Did you enjoy the cupcake baking competition? Why or why not?
- What is the most important learning you experienced as a result of the class?

After Ms. Hutchings completes all three of the focus group sessions, she will be ready to prepare for her new classes!

RESEARCH SCENARIO 5

Purple Blossom Middle School serves a large number of students who use power wheelchairs, or power chairs, because of a disability. As such, the school has a very competitive Power Soccer team, The Purple Blossom Hornets (for information on Power Soccer, see http://www.powersoccerusa.org). Students with disabilities at Purple Blossom have the opportunity to become involved in a staff-student mentoring program. Various staff members and students with disabilities opt in to the program and are paired together based on common interests. The pairs meet periodically to talk about school. The purpose of the program is to help students with disabilities feel at home and welcomed at Purple Blossom. Mr. Bluefish, who oversees the mentoring program, has heard from several of the staff members regarding some of their mentees sentiments. The students with disabilities are interested in hosting some type of educational program for the rest of the student body. These students are primarily interested in helping able-bodied students understand what it's like to use a power chair. Furthermore, the Hornets' Power Soccer team wants to increase attendance at their home games, especially their upcoming championship tournament. Mr. Bluefish had an idea: provide the power chair users with a camera and ask them to document various aspects of their lives through photography. After taking the photographs, the power chair users then engage in focus groups and generate narrations, or captions, for their images. Finally, the photographs and captions would be combined and made into a photo exhibition. The entire school and surrounding community will be invited to the exhibition.

RESEARCH WORDS

Qualitative research (noun): "An approach to social science research that emphasizes collecting descriptive data in natural settings, uses inductive thinking, and emphasizes understanding the [participant's] point of view" (Bogdan & Biklen, 2007, p. 274).

Fieldwork (noun): Work done in the field of research such as exploration, observations, and interviews.

Interview (noun and verb): A meeting in which one or more individuals ask questions of and/or converse with another person or persons about a topic (noun); to have a meeting with another individual to ask questions or converse about a topic (verb).

Observation (noun): An act or instance of watching, perceiving, and/or noticing attentively.

Ethnography (noun): A branch of anthropology that consists of the systematic description of individual cultures; a written product consisting of a systematic description of an individual culture.

Culture (noun): A group of individuals who all share the same or similar ways of living with regard to values, behaviors, language, dress, food, symbols, and so forth.

Interpret (verb): To provide meaning.

Quantitative research (noun): An approach to social science research that emphasizes systematically investigating a topic, such as a social phenomenon, via statistical or computational techniques.

Generalize (verb): To form general principles or opinions; to infer that the results from one group or sample involved in a research study apply to other, similar groups or samples.

Researcher bias (noun): A particular tendency or inclination had by an individual conducting research.

Population (noun): A large and defined group of individuals from which a smaller group of individuals is recruited or selected to participate in a research study.

Sample (noun): A group of individuals involved in a research study.

Control group (noun): A collection of individuals involved in a research study that is not exposed to treatment and to which the experimental group is compared.

Experimental group (noun): A collection of individuals in a research study that is exposed to treatment and to which the control group is compared.

Variable (noun): A changeable feature or factor such as age or weight.

Data (noun): Items of information. (*Note*: data is plural; datum is singular.)

Predict (verb): To assert in advance.

Reliability (noun): The degree to which an instrument yields the same results during repeated trials.

Validity (noun): The degree to which an instrument measures what it is meant to measure.

Statistics (noun): Numerical facts or data themselves.

Replicate (verb): To repeat.

Cause (noun): A reason or motive.

Effect (noun): Something produced by a cause; consequence.

Correlation (noun): A mutual relation of two or more things.

Analysis (noun): A study of the nature of something and the determination of its elemental parts and their relationships to one another.

I HAVE/WHO HAS? CARDS

FINISH: I have **ANALYSIS**.

START: Who has an approach to social science research that emphasizes collecting descriptive data in natural settings, uses inductive thinking, and emphasizes understanding the [participant's] point of view?

I have **QUALITATIVE RESEARCH**.

Who has work done in the field of research such as exploration, observations, and interviews?

I have **FIELDWORK**.

Who has a meeting in which one or more individuals ask questions of and/or converse with another person or persons about a topic (noun), or to have a meeting with another individual to ask questions or converse about a topic (verb)?

I have **INTERVIEW**.

Who has an act or instance of watching, perceiving, and/or noticing attentively?

I have **OBSERVATION**.

Who has a branch of anthropology that consists of the systematic description of individual cultures, or a written product consisting of a systematic description of an individual culture?

I have **ETHNOGRAPHY**.

Who has a group of individuals who all share the same or similar ways of living with regard to values, behaviors, language, dress, food, symbols, and so forth?

I have **CULTURE**.

Who has to provide meaning?

I have **INTERPRET**.

Who has an approach to social science research that emphasizes systematically investigating a topic, such as a social phenomenon, via statistical or computational techniques?

I have **QUANTITATIVE RESEARCH**.

Who has to form general principles or opinions; to infer that the results from one group or sample involved in a research study apply to other, similar groups or samples?

I have **GENERALIZE**.

Who has a particular tendency or inclination had by an individual conducting research?

I have **RESEARCHER BIAS**.

Who has a large and defined group of individuals from which a smaller group of individuals is recruited or selected to participate in a research study?

I have **POPULATION**.

Who has a group of individuals involved in a research study?

I have **SAMPLE**.

Who has a collection of individuals involved in a research study that is not exposed to treatment and to which the experimental group is compared?

I have **CONTROL GROUP**.

Who has a collection of individuals in a research study that is exposed to treatment and to which the control group is compared?

I have **EXPERIMENTAL GROUP**.

Who has a changeable feature or factor such as age or weight?

I have **VARIABLE**.

Who has items of information?

I have **DATA**.

Who has to assert in advance?

I have **PREDICT**.

Who has the degree to which an instrument yields the same results during repeated trials?

I have **RELIABILITY**.

Who has the degree to which an instrument measures what it is meant to measure?

I have **VALIDITY**.

Who has numerical facts or data themselves?

I have **STATISTICS**.

Who has to repeat?

I have **REPLICATE**.

Who has a reason or motive?

I have **CAUSE**.

Who has something produced by a cause, or consequence?

I have **EFFECT**.

Who has a mutual relation of two or more things?

I have **CORRELATION**.

Who has the study of the nature of something and the determination of its elemental parts and their relationships to one another?

Name:_____ Date: _____

EXIT CARD

1. In your own words, describe the differences between quantitative and qualitative research.

2. After this lesson, about which aspects of quantitative and/or qualitative research do you want to learn more?

3. What lingering questions do you still have about quantitative and qualitative research?

PREPARATORY LESSON 3

What Is Action Research?

Preparation

Purpose: To understand the concept of action research.

Students Will Know:
- **Action research** (noun): "An investigation conducted by the person or the people empowered to take action concerning their own actions, for the purpose of improving their future actions" (Sagor, 2005, p. 4); "a form of research that is conducted by practitioners" (Glanz, 1998, p. 20); "a systematic approach to investigation that enables people to find effective solutions to problems they confront in their everyday lives" (Stringer, 2007, p. 1).

Students Will Understand:
- the concept of action research and how it is different from traditional research.

Students Will Be Able To:
- implement and carry out a small-scale action research project.

Instructional Strategies Used:
- Guided inquiry
- Whole-group discussion
- Small-group work
- Mind mapping/storyboarding

Materials Needed:
- Copies of Executive Summary of Action Research Plan handout
- Newsprint
- Markers and/or colored pencils

Implementation

Time Needed: 60–80 minutes

Instructions:

- Start the lesson by asking the students to think about the word *action*. Ask them to describe what this word means. Guide the students toward a definition of action that is emblematic of something done, performed, accomplished, or carried out. Then prompt them to think about the phrase *action research*. Ask them to articulate their definitions in a whole-group guided discussion. Explain to the students that action research implies that something is "done" with the results or findings of a research study. In other words, action research is a form of systematic inquiry that is followed by taking action in accordance with the results or findings of the research.

- Ask the students to think about how action research is different from traditional research. You may also want to ask the students about how they define traditional research. They can discuss this in small groups or as a whole class. Glanz (1998) noted that action research differs from traditional research in three important ways: (a) action research is often more simplistic than traditional research (i.e., action research does not typically involve complex statistical analyses, and it is typically associated with qualitative research), (b) action research is often used by practitioners to solve specific problems in everyday life, and (c) action research is not generalizable to other settings. Present these unique characteristics to the students. Ask the students to think about specific examples of the differentiating factors or put the list in their own words.

- Pose these questions to students: *Who does traditional research? Who benefits from traditional research? Who knows about traditional research?* Traditional research is typically done within institutions of higher education, research laboratories, businesses, or government entities. Trained researchers typically conduct this type of research. Much research is disseminated through academic journals, white papers, conference presentations, or other formal and academic means; it is meant to advance the creation of new knowledge, usually for the sake of building on the existing knowledge base. Oftentimes, only a small segment of the overall public is privy to traditional research. Because it is typically written in disciplinary jargon, it can be difficult to consume. The individuals who undertake action research, those who benefit from it, and those who consume it are much different from individuals involved with traditional research. Ask the students to think of some examples.

- Engage the students in a simulation. Divide the class into groups. Ask each group to invent the following: a fictional town, a fictional problem or point of tension within the town, a fictional community organization within the town charged with addressing the problem or tension point, and three fictional people who work within the organization. When the group has completed this, ask them to draft a small-scale action research plan to be carried out by the organization, including specific tasks for the three fictional people to complete.

- Provide each group with a large piece of newsprint. Ask them to draw or sketch out the various elements of the simulation (town and so on) along with their action research plan. The students might think of the exercise as creating a mind-map or a storyboard.

- Once each group has completed their work on the newsprint, provide them with the Executive Summary of Action Research Plan worksheet. Each group should complete the worksheet based upon their work within the simulation.

- Provide each group with about 5–10 minutes to present their plans to the whole class. After each presentation, engage the whole class in discussion about the presenting group's plan.

- Engage the whole group in guided inquiry about the methods they each selected for their plan. Use the following questions to facilitate a guided discussion:

  o What methods did you select (e.g., focus groups, observations, surveys, interviews)?

  o Why did you select those methods?

  o Based on what you'd like to know, are those methods best?

  o How much data will you collect? Will it be too little, or too much?

  o How will you analyze or understand the data (i.e., How will you move from data to results or findings?)?

- Ask the groups to brainstorm ways in which their findings or results might "look" (e.g., what does survey data "look like"?) and how those findings or results might be translated into action. For example, if their town has an underused public community park because of lack of upkeep, what might the students propose be done to bolster use? Some solutions might be to create a coalition of volunteers to mow, mulch, and pick up litter; a fundraising coalition to support the implementation of trash cans, trash service, and Dogipots ® (http://www.dogipot.com); or a coalition to create a social media presence for the park to advertise events, reservation procedures, and policies.

Differentiation

- Ask students to search online to discover a real-world community problem or point of tension. This can be from a community anywhere in the world. Encourage students to locate communities and concomitant community problems or tension points within areas they have visited or would like to visit.

- Have the students create an action research plan to better understand the history, implications, and possible causes of the problem or tension point.

- Encourage the students to peer review, edit, and refine their plans. Have the students locate contact information for a stakeholder within the community who may be in a position to address the problem or tension point through action research. Ask the students to compose a professional letter or e-mail message to the identified stakeholder. This correspondence should serve as a cover letter for the students' action research plans. Review the students' work and encourage them to actually send the correspondence and plan if you feel it is appropriate.

- If a student receives correspondence back from the stakeholder, be sure to include the whole class in a discussion of the outreach! Talk with the students about how what they learn in school can and should be applicable to their lives outside of school and the world around them.

- As time allows, encourage students to think about and explore funding for their action research plans. Action research can be expensive, and it requires human labor. How will these expenses be paid? Encourage the students to explore granting agencies online. Challenge them to identify a funding agency that might support their proposed plan.

Name:_____ Date: _____

EXECUTIVE SUMMARY OF ACTION RESEARCH PLAN

Describe your town.

Describe the fictional problem or point of tension within the town.

Describe the fictional community organization charged with addressing the problem or point of tension within the town.

Describe the three fictional organization members who will carry out the action research plan.

Name:	Name:	Name:

Describe your action research plan.

Outline the tasks to be accomplished by the three organization members described above.

Community Organization Member	Action Research Tasks

PREPARATORY LESSON 4

Why Is Research Important?

Preparation

Purpose: To understand why research is important.

Students Will Know*:*
- **Claim** (noun or verb): An assertion of something as a fact (noun); to make such an assertion (verb).
- **Evidence** (noun or verb): That which proves or disproves something (noun); to offer proof of something (verb).

Students Will Understand:
- the importance of research and how research is the basis for the creation of the world's knowledge.

Students Will Be Able To:
- articulate why research is important, as it underpins important aspects of daily life such as decision making, problem solving, and knowing.

Instructional Strategies Used:
- Guided inquiry
- Whole-group discussion
- Small-group work
- Video analysis
- Web searching

Materials Needed:
- Career Cards (duplicate based on number of students in the class)
- Career Card worksheets
- Copies of Video Analysis handout
- A computer with Internet access

Implementation

Purpose: To gain understanding of the importance of research.

Time Needed: 60 minutes (all parts)

Instructions:
Part 1
- Start the lesson by asking the students to think about the importance of research of all kinds. How has research affected their lives? If further probing is needed, pose the following questions:
  o How do you think your toothpaste was developed? In what ways might this development have involved research?
  o Why do most vehicles have airbags? How did car designers know airbags might help save lives in the event of a car accident?
  o How do we know texting and driving is an unsafe combination?
  o If you have a sprained ankle, your doctor, athletic trainer, or coach might advise you to use the RICE method: rest, ice, compression, and elevation. How do they know the RICE method leads to (a faster) recovery?

- Next, ask the students to each think about what they'd like to be when they grow up. Encourage them to be specific. For example, if a student would like to be a game designer, ask what types of games he or she would like to design, such as smartphone apps, multiuser computer games, board games, or puzzles.
- Ask the students how research might be part of their future careers. Will research be a part of their day-to-day work? If the student works for a company or a school, will the analysis of data, versus the collection of data, become one of their tasks? Facilitate this discussion as a whole group until some different types of examples are shared.
- Have students pick a Career Card. Ask students to complete the card individually. Once they have completed their cards, have the students get into groups based on their cards. Two to four students should be in each group, depending on the size of your class. While in groups, the students should transpose their card ideas onto the full-sized Career Card worksheets, thus integrating all group members' ideas. At this point, they may also use the Internet to gain a better understand of what is involved in each career.
- Finally, ask each group to briefly present their combined work to the rest of the class.

Part 2

- Use YouTube to preselect a number of television commercials to present to the class. Each commercial should advertise some type of product, such as laundry detergent, motor oil, toothpaste, paper towels, deodorant, or cleaning supplies.
- Provide students with Video Analysis worksheets (one per video).
- Go over the questions on the worksheet. Students may need assistance with the terms *claims* and *evidence*. Engage in a discussion about these two related terms (see the Students Will Know section of this lesson for definitions).
- Show the students one video and ask them to complete a Video Analysis worksheet based on the commercial. You may need to show the commercial a number of times so students can fully analyze the video.
- Once students have completed the worksheet, engage them in a guided conversation about what they noticed while watching.
- Guide the students toward a conversation about the importance of research in everyday life. With a critical eye, students can begin to notice the ubiquity of research all around them.
- Repeat this process with the students a few times with different commercials. Try to locate commercials that showcase different types of products.
- Finally, ask students the question, "Why is research important?" Research, in all of its forms, lays the foundation for knowledge.

Differentiation

- Ask the students to brainstorm a new product to sell. If students need assistance with product design, encourage them to consider their interests. For example, if students have pets or play sports or musical instruments, ask them to think about their lingering needs. Can some product meet those needs?
- Have the students create both a written narration as well as a drawing of the product. The product could take many forms. Encourage students to be as creative as possible.
- Next, ask the students to develop a research plan through which they will develop the product. In other words, once they have a concept, they must then begin to develop the final product through a cyclical process of research—research-design-research-design—repeating until they design the final product (see Figure 1).

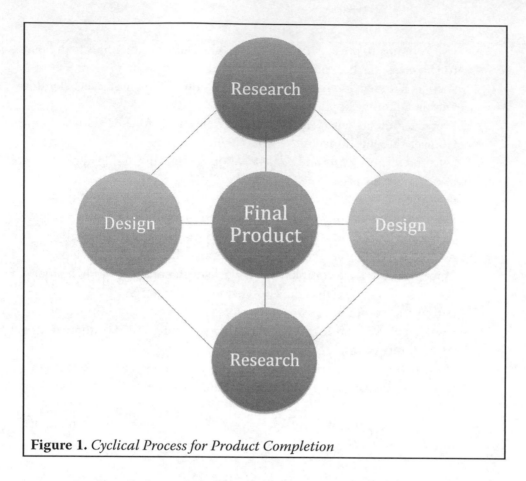

Figure 1. *Cyclical Process for Product Completion*

- Finally, ask the students to create a marketing plan for the product. This might include establishment of the target market, logo design, social media presence, television commercials, brochures, online advertisements, and so on.
- If the students are interested, allow them to work together to bring a panel of local business professionals into the school for a mock product-pitching session. Have the students prepare presentations for the panel outlining their ideas and plans. Encourage the students to highlight the utilization of research within their process. Ask the business professionals to engage the students in discussion about their ideas and plans.

Name:_____ Date: _____

CAREER CARDS

Veterinarian What roles does research play in this career?	**Social Media Consultant** What roles does research play in this career?	**Environmental Scientist** What roles does research play in this career?
Nurse What roles does research play in this career?	**Magazine Writer** What roles does research play in this career?	**Chemical Engineer** What roles does research play in this career?
Restaurant Owner What roles does research play in this career?	**High School Teacher** What roles does research play in this career?	**Landscaper** What roles does research play in this career?

VETERINARIAN

What roles does research play in this career?

Name:_____ Date: _____

SOCIAL MEDIA CONSULTANT

What roles does research play in this career?

ENVIRONMENTAL SCIENTIST

What roles does research play in this career?

NURSE

What roles does research play in this career?

MAGAZINE WRITER

What roles does research play in this career?

CHEMICAL ENGINEER

What roles does research play in this career?

RESTAURANT OWNER

What roles does research play in this career?

Name:_____   Date: _____

HIGH SCHOOL TEACHER

What roles does research play in this career?

LANDSCAPER

What roles does research play in this career?

ACTION RESEARCH FOR KIDS © PRUFROCK PRESS

VIDEO ANALYSIS

did the commercial put forward about the product?

mmercial put forward to substantiate (i.e., back up) the claims?

fficient for the claim? Why or why not?

e came?

oduct, how would you go about creating evidence?

Section 3
Quantitative Research

Unit 1
Survey Research

This unit is designed to teach students the process of doing survey research.

What You Will Find in This Unit

PRETEACHING LESSON

What Are Surveys?

Preparation

Purpose: To understand survey research.

Students Will Know:

- **Survey** (noun and verb): A tool to gather information from a sample of individuals about something that interests the researcher (noun); to use your survey to gather information (verb).
- **Data** (noun): Items of information. (*Note*: data is plural; datum is singular.)
- **Tally** (verb): To count the marks you made when you collected your data.
- **Tally mark** (noun): A mark to keep count of the answers to your survey.
- **Graph** (noun and verb): A diagram to show your data visually (noun); the process used to display your information on a graph (verb).
- **Sample** (noun): A group of individuals involved in a research study.
- **Population** (noun): A large and defined group of individuals from which a smaller group of individuals is recruited or selected to participate in a research study.
- **Open-ended** (adjective): A type of survey question that allows respondents to provide any answer they choose.
- **Closed** (adjective): A type of survey question that requires respondents to choose an answer from several choices.
- **Respondent** (noun): A person who replies to a survey.
- **Rating scale** (noun): A scale used when the researcher wants the respondent to select a choice from several options that vary by degree, either quantitatively or qualitatively.

Students Will Understand:

- that an individual can be an agent of change by using a survey to collect opinions and preferences from a sample of individuals about a particular topic or problem and then using that information to demonstrate the group's preferences and opinions to policy makers;
- that, when conducting a survey, there are ethical issues that must be considered such as anonymity, respect, and privacy; and
- that graphs can help make organizing data easier.

Students Will Be Able To:
- design a survey, including determining a sample population and writing a closed survey question;
- administer a survey, collect and analyze data, display the data in a meaningful way, and use the data to make a change; and
- explain the importance of ethics in survey research.

Instructional Strategies Used:
- Guided inquiry
- Exit cards

Materials Needed:
- Clipboards
- Examples of surveys
- Copies of Exit Card handout

Resources:
- *Scammed by Statistics* by Edward Zaccaro and Daniel Zaccaro

Implementation

Time Needed: Varies

Instructions:
- Explain to the students what a survey is by saying something like this: "A survey is a tool to gather information from a sample of individuals about something that interests the researcher. For example, I want to find out how many students have read each of the *Harry Potter* books. I need to design my question to ask to everyone in the class to gather that information. I could ask, 'Which Harry Potter books have you read? When I read the name of a Harry Potter book, tell me if you have read it.' I would then make a list of the seven Harry Potter books, go to each student in our class, and ask my question. I would make a tally mark for each book the person has read, and then I would move to the next person and repeat the procedure. Once I've asked the questions to everyone, I can tally the marks for each book. Now I have a set of data to organize in a way that helps me answer my question about how many students have read each book."
- Show students Table 1, explain how the table is set up, and identify the tally marks.

Table 1

A Survey of Students Who Have Read Each Harry Potter Book

Name of Book	Number of Students Who Have Read It
Harry Potter and the Sorceror's Stone	|||||||||||||||||||||||||
Harry Potter and the Chamber of Secrets	||||||||||||||||
Harry Potter and the Prisoner of Azkaban	||||||||||
Harry Potter and the Goblet of Fire	||||||||
Harry Potter and the Order of the Phoenix	||||||||
Harry Potter and the Half-Blood Prince	|||||
Harry Potter and the Deathly Hallows	|||||

- Explain to students that surveys can be used to gather input about preferences, too. For example, tell your students, "The PTA has raised money to add a new piece of equipment to the playground. They want to know what the students would prefer: a big slide, a jungle gym, or a climbing wall. They have designed a survey asking students to circle the name of the one piece of equipment that they prefer. Once they gather all of the surveys from the students and tally the votes, they discover that the students prefer a climbing wall. Based on the data, the PTA parents purchase and install a climbing wall on the playground."

- When you've finished explaining, consider asking the students to sketch out how a table for this survey might look. This is a good formative assessment.

- Discuss with students that survey questions can be open-ended or closed. Now would be a good time to introduce those vocabulary words. Open-ended questions allow the respondents to choose their responses— for example, *What is your favorite sport?* Closed questions (sometimes called closed-ended or fixed response questions) ask the respondents to choose their answer from a list of choices. For example, *Do you think the school should change the school dismissal time from 2 p.m. to 3 p.m.?* Respondents would answer either yes or no. Sometimes we offer more than just two choices. One way to do this is to provide several answers, such as *What is your favorite ice cream flavor: chocolate, vanilla, strawberry, or butter pecan?* We can also ask questions that work well on a rating scale. For example, consider this question: *How important is it to have a daily dessert choice at lunch?* We could make a rating scale like this:

1	2	3	4
Not at all important	Not very important	A little bit important	Very important

Respondents would circle the number that best matched how important it was to them to have a daily dessert choice at lunch.

- You should have a discussion about ethics and confidentiality with your students at a level appropriate to their development. Even young children can understand being sensitive so that they don't hurt someone's feelings. The discussion can cover topics about dealing with sensitive issues and politically charged issues, for example. We want the students to understand the need to be friendly and to show appreciation for the time the respondents spent to answer the students' questions. The words *please* and *thank you* are essential vocabulary for those doing survey research!

- Once you have completed the discussion, distribute the Exit Card handout for students to complete. After all of the cards are returned, sort through their responses to see if there are any students who need to review the material.

Differentiation

- Work with students who do not understand the concepts and need further review before you start the next lesson. Those with a clear understanding can independently work on other forms of questions, such as ranking questions, while you work with these students. Otherwise, provide some anchoring activities while you are reteaching your small group.

Name: _____ Date: _____

EXIT CARD

1. What is a survey?

2. Think of one question you would like to ask your classmates. Write it here.

3. Design a closed survey question to find the answer to the question you wrote above.

LESSON 1

Who Are We?

Preparation

Purpose: To gain practice in creating a survey, collecting data, analyzing the results, and presenting the findings.

Students Will Understand:
- that a survey can help us gain a better understanding of a group of individuals;
- that, when conducting a survey, there are ethical issues that must be considered such as anonymity, respect, and privacy; and
- that graphs can help make organizing data easier.

Students Will Be Able To:
- develop a question to use to focus their research;
- design a survey based on their question to gather information about their classmates; and
- administer the survey, collect and analyze the data, and display the data in a meaningful way.

Instructional Strategies Used:
- Guided inquiry

Materials Needed:
- A copy of Loreen Leedy's *The Great Graph Contest*
- Clipboards
- Examples of surveys
- Chart paper, poster board for displaying data
- Microsoft Excel or other software for making graphs (if developmentally appropriate for your students)
- Document camera
- Copies or visual display of Writing Your Survey Question From Your Research Question handout
- Copies or visual display of How to Introduce Yourself and Your Survey handout
- Copies or visual display of A Finished Product handout

Resources:
- *Exploring Statistics in the Elementary Grades: Book One, Grades K–6* by Carolyn Bereska, L. Carey Bolster, Cyrilla A. Bolster, and Richard Schaeffer
- *Exploring Statistics in the Elementary Grades: Book Two, Grades 4–8* by Carolyn Bereska, L. Carey Bolster, Cyrilla A. Bolster, and Richard Schaeffer
- *Probability, Statistics & Graphing, Grades 2–3* by Tina Szmadzinski
- *Probability, Statistics & Graphing, Grades 4–5* by Tina Szmadzinski

Implementation

Time Needed: Varies

Instructions:
- Review the previous lesson. Read *The Great Graph Contest* to the class as an introduction to this lesson. Although this is an elementary grade book, older students will still enjoy the story. It will provide a fun way to jog students' memories about graphing.
- Explain to the students that they will be working like researchers today. They will determine the question about their classmates to which they want answers, create surveys to answer the question, gather their data, analyze the results, and display the information on a graph.
- Have students brainstorm information that interests them. Some typical responses would be movies, sports, video games, technology, food, leisure activities, allowance amounts, pets, brands of clothing, superheroes/heroines, cartoons, television shows, vacation plans, and so forth.
- Students may choose a research topic from the list or go with their own ideas. Have students get your approval once they have written their research questions. Do not allow questions from different students to be identical. It is fine to have the same topic, but insist that questions are designed to tap different areas. For example, if the category is video games, one student could ask opinions about preferences for video games (*Which video games do you like?*) while another could gather data on how much time students engage in video gaming each week (*How much time do you spend playing video games each week?*). Have students write their survey question(s) from their research question and make sure they get their survey question(s) approved.
- Display the Writing Your Survey Question From Your Research Question handout for students, so that those who need a model will have access to one.

- Once questions are approved, check to see if students need your assistance in copying surveys for distribution. Students who are tallying answers will only need their copy of the survey. Have students design their own surveys, including how they will introduce themselves and their survey. Make sure they understand how to collect the data. Display the How to Introduce Yourself and Your Survey handout for those who need a model.

- Distribute clipboards to all students so that they have a hard surface to use when gathering their data. Have them place their surveys on the clipboards unless they are distributing the survey individually. Determine a schedule so that each student has adequate time to collect data.

- Once data have been collected, allow students time to analyze their data and create an appropriate graph. Observe students as they work and offer assistance and support as needed. The A Finished Product handout shows what a completed product might look like.

Differentiation

- If students need a minilesson or refresher about making graphs, the materials in the Resources section can help solidify students' understanding.

- As an extension, you might want to bind the various products into a class book titled *Who Are We?* Each page will provide data that tells about your class, their likes and dislikes, what they do in their free time, and so forth. Alternatively, you could prepare a bulletin board display with the products. Some students who show great interest in this activity might try to describe the "typical" student in your class. You can also incorporate the data into class discussions when appropriate—for example, looking at data about food during a discussion of good nutrition.

WRITING A SURVEY QUESTION FROM YOUR RESEARCH QUESTION

Research Question: What kind of candy do my classmates prefer?

An Open-Ended Survey Question:
What is your favorite candy?

Or

A Closed Survey Question:
From the list below, place an "X" by the name of your favorite candy:

_____ M&Ms—plain	_____ Skittles	_____ Jolly Ranchers	_____ Nerds
_____ M&Ms—peanut	_____ Life Savers	_____ Starbursts	_____ Junior Mints

HOW TO INTRODUCE YOURSELF AND YOUR SURVEY

1. **Greet the person and explain what you are doing.**
   "Hello. My name is [*state your name*], and I am trying to find out about [*state your topic*]. I want to answer this question: [*state your research question*]."

2. **Politely ask the person if he or she will participate in your survey.**
   "Do you have time to participate in my survey?"

3. **State your survey question.**
   If it is an open-ended question, ask the person to give an answer, and then you write the answer on your sheet. If it is a closed question, give the person each choice and ask him or her to select one of the choices. Put a tally mark by the selected choice.

4. **Thank the person for assisting you.**
   "Thank you so much for participating in my research."

5. **Repeat Steps 1–4 for each person that you survey.**

A FINISHED PRODUCT

Research Question: What kind of candy do my classmates prefer?

Survey Question: From the list below, tell me which is your favorite candy?

Tallied Data: Number of students who preferred each kind of candy:

9 M&Ms—plain	**5** Skittles	**3** Jolly Ranchers	**3** Nerds
5 M&Ms—peanut	**3** Life Savers	**2** Starbursts	**0** Junior Mints

Graph: *Number of Students Who Preferred Each Kind of Candy*

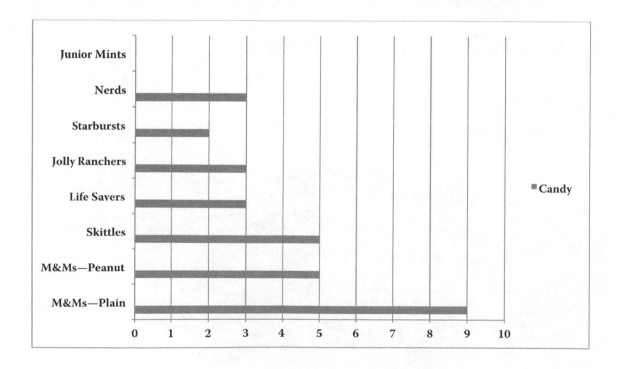

ACTION RESEARCH FOR KIDS © PRUFROCK PRESS

LESSON 2

Survey Data Everywhere

Preparation

Purpose: To understand the impact of survey data in everyday life.

Students Will Know:
- **Valid** (adjective): Acceptable.

Students Will Understand:
- that a survey can help us gain a better understanding of a group of individuals, and
- that surveys are used by companies and individuals who want to better understand a group of individuals, particularly their likes, dislikes, and opinions about a product, issue, or topic.

Students Will Be Able To:
- find examples of surveys in everyday use, judge whether the surveys were implemented ethically, and evaluate whether the survey results are valid.

Instructional Strategies Used:
- Guided inquiry

Materials Needed:
- Computers with Internet access
- Television
- Newspapers
- Magazines
- Chart paper

Resources:
- Surveys for kids can be found at the following websites:
  - Scholastic (http://teacher.scholastic.com/kidusasu)
  - About.com (http://homeschooling.about.com/od/freeprintables/ss/surveyprint.htm)
  - HowStuffWorks (http://communication.howstuffworks.com/how-online-surveys-work4.htm)

- The "Survey Says" section at the end of episodes of *Family Feud* is also a good resource. Use YouTube to search for videos, but preview them first to be sure the episodes are appropriate for your students.

Implementation

Time Needed: Varies

Instructions:
- In this lesson, students are going to find examples of surveys, review claims made by the group that developed and analyzed the survey, and judge whether or not we should believe the claims that are made.
- Ask students if they have seen or heard any claims based on survey data. After the students have discussed what they have heard, discuss whether they believe the claims. It would be a good idea to have an example handy in case they can't think of one—for example, *3 out of 4 dentists recommend Crest*. Gather their ideas on chart paper and review their suggestions with them. Use these ideas to create a rubric for the students to use in judging the validity of the survey claims they find in the next part of the lesson. Discuss how to be sure the survey is ethical. You may need to review the Preteaching Lesson for this unit for those who need help determining whether or not the survey was ethical.
- Provide students with newspapers, magazines, and access to television, the Internet, and any other place where they might find examples of claims based on statistical analysis. Distribute copies of the rubric that was created based on their earlier discussion. Allow ample time for them to review 3–5 examples and to complete the rubric on each. Bring the class back together to discuss their results. Lead students in a discussion about what information is important to include so that others have a basis to judge the validity of their own survey results.
- Make sure students have a good understanding of the issues in this lesson before they go to Lesson 3.

Differentiation

- For students who have a more sophisticated understanding about the validity of survey results, you may want them to discuss among themselves while you lead the rest of the class in a more basic discussion (see Implementation, Step 3). Those who are more advanced may want to delve into the topic of reliability, too.

LESSON 3

Survey Monkey-ing Around

Preparation

Purpose: To understand how to use a tool for creating online surveys.

Students Will Know:
- **Online survey** (noun): A survey that is designed, distributed, and analyzed electronically.

Students Will Understand:
- that surveys may be designed, implemented, and analyzed online.

Students Will Be Able To:
- design and distribute a survey online using SurveyMonkey, and
- collect the data and analyze the results.

Instructional Strategies Used:
- Guided inquiry

Materials Needed:
- Computers with Internet access

Resources:
- SurveyMonkey User Manual (http://s3.amazonaws.com/SurveyMonkey Files/UserManual.pdf)

Implementation

Time Needed: Varies

Instructions:
- Review previous lessons. Have students explain why surveys are used, pros and cons, ethical practice, and so forth.
- Explain that they will be designing surveys to use online.

- Access the SurveyMonkey website (http://www.surveymonkey.com). Explain that SurveyMonkey is a private company that allows anyone to create, distribute, and analyze a survey of no more than 10 questions online, free of charge. To use SurveyMonkey, the people you are interested in surveying must have an e-mail address.
- Have students assist you in developing a survey that you could send to the whole class. Project your computer screen so everyone can view the process. If you need assistance, there are tutorials on the website and a help manual (see the Resources section, above). Make sure students see how you access these documents in case they need them later.
- See A Survey Created Using SurveyMonkey for an example survey for the classroom.

Differentiation

- Know your students—if they are not developmentally ready for this kind of research, you may omit this lesson.

A SURVEY CREATED USING SURVEYMONKEY

Survey about Reading

1. I am a

⚪ boy

⚪ girl

2. When I have free time, I choose to read a book

⚪ always

⚪ usually

⚪ sometimes

⚪ rarely

⚪ never

3. When I have to read a book, my favorite kind of book is

⚪ nonfiction

⚪ fiction

4. When I have to read a nonfiction book, I usually choose

⚪ biographies

⚪ how-to books

⚪ books about a particular topic such as animals or sports

5. When I have to read a fiction book, I usually choose

⚪ mysteries

⚪ stories with girls as the main characters

⚪ stories with boys as the main characters

⚪ action/adventure books

⚪ science fiction

⚪ fantasy

ACTION LESSON 1

Cookies in the Cafeteria

Preparation

Purpose: To provide students with a real-world opportunity to demonstrate how gathering, analyzing, and interpreting data, then using the results to foster a change, can impact the lives of children.

Students Will Understand:
- that a survey can help us gain a better understanding of a group of individuals;
- that, when conducting a survey, there are ethical issues that must be considered such as anonymity, respect, and privacy; and
- that graphs can help make organizing data easier.

Students Will Be Able To:
- show their young friends at Edgewood School how to effect a change in the kinds of cookies offered daily by the school cafeteria.

Instructional Strategies Used:
- Guided inquiry

Materials Needed:
- Copies of Cookies in the Cafeteria handout

Implementation

Time Needed: 2–4 days

Instructions:
- Students will develop a survey to gather data, pilot the survey with your school, analyze and interpret the results, and show their friends how to display the data to make a strong case for change.
- The scenario is meant as a guide. You can put your own spin on it by changing the location to your own school and determining a particular

change your students would like to make. Letting the students have ownership of the activity can increase student interest and engagement. For example, perhaps students want (or don't want!) healthy snacks in the vending machines or a longer recess period.

- Be sure that students practice the skills they learned in Lessons 1–3. Students can work in groups or individually. As students work, wander around the room listening to discussions and checking student work. When you find a student or group that is straying, bring them back to the task. When you find misconceptions or misinterpretations, make the corrections in an on-the-spot minilesson.
- Students can display data and support their argument through a PowerPoint or Prezi presentation, poster, persuasive letter, or a host of other means. Help students polish their presentations when necessary. Provide students with a rubric for the project; the DAP Tool for Technical Reports (see pp. 49-51) have been provided as examples.
- *Note:* The authors would like to thank Dr. Thalia Mulvihill for her inspiration for this lesson and scenario in particular.

COOKIES IN THE CAFETERIA

Dear Mrs. Smith's class,

Mr. Johnson, the principal of Edgewood Elementary School, loves oatmeal cookies. He loves them so much that he eats at least one every day, generally for lunch. Consequently, the cafeteria's only choice for anyone wanting a cookie for dessert at lunch is oatmeal. I think that students might like other choices. My friend Jason's mother packs him chocolate chip cookies, and Tonya's grandmother always packs a snickerdoodle cookie for Tonya to have with her lunch.

We think it would be a great idea if we could have several kinds of cookies to choose from at lunch. Jason, Tonya, and I talked to Mr. Johnson about this. He said he thought everyone wanted oatmeal, but he would need proof that other cookies were popular choices. He didn't want to offer cookies that no one would eat. Mr. Johnson said he thought you would have an idea about how we could figure this out. Can you help us?

Sincerely,
Eve Morgan

TECHNICAL REPORT TIER 1—DAP TOOL

CONTENT	▪ Is the content correct and complete?	0 1 2 3 4 5 6
	▪ Has the content been thought about in a way that goes beyond a surface understanding?	0 1 2 3 4 5 6
	▪ Is the content put together in such a way that people understand it?	0 1 2 3 4 5 6
PRESENTATION		
FORM	▪ Does the title describe the main idea? Is the topic clearly stated early in the paper? Do strong transitions lead from one section to another? Does each section have one main idea? Does it come to a close and link back to the topic?	0 1 2 3 4 5 6
DETAIL	▪ Is there enough detail to prove the points? Does all information relate to the main idea? Are the ideas fully explained and supported? Are all figures and graphs explained well?	0 1 2 3 4 5 6
Style	▪ Is it written for the expected audience? Are the words clear and concise? Has slang been avoided and all jargon explained? Are the sentences straightforward and clear? Is it written in active voice and third person? Are tables used to organize data when appropriate?	0 1 2 3 4 5 6
LAYOUT	▪ Do headings help the audience understand the upcoming section? Are important diagrams, charts, illustrations, or tables included and explained? Are units included with all data? Is the layout consistent as to font, bullets, underlining, and so forth?	0 1 2 3 4 5 6
CREATIVITY	▪ Is the content seen in a new way?	0 1 2 3 4 5 6
	▪ Is the presentation done in a new way?	0 1 2 3 4 5 6
REFLECTION	▪ What did you learn about the content as you completed this product?	0 1 2 3 4 5 6
	▪ What did you learn about yourself as a learner by creating this product?	0 1 2 3 4 5 6

Comments

Meaning of Performance Scale:

6—PROFESSIONAL LEVEL: level expected from a professional in the content area

5—ADVANCED LEVEL: level exceeds expectations of the standard

4—PROFICIENT LEVEL: level expected for meeting the standard

3—PROGRESSING LEVEL: level demonstrates movement toward the standard

2—NOVICE LEVEL: level demonstrates initial awareness and knowledge of standard

1—NONPERFORMING LEVEL: level indicates no effort made to meet standard

0—NONPARTICIPATING LEVEL: level indicates nothing turned in

Note. Adapted from *Strategies for Differentiating Instruction: Best Practices for the Classroom* (2nd ed.; p. 211), by J. L. Roberts and T. F. Inman, 2007, Waco, TX: Prufrock Press. Copyright © 2007 by Prufrock Press. Adapted with permission.

TECHNICAL REPORT TIER 2—DAP TOOL

CONTENT	▪ Content is accurate.	0 1 2 3 4 5 6
	▪ Content has depth and complexity of thought.	0 1 2 3 4 5 6
	▪ Content is organized.	0 1 2 3 4 5 6
PRESENTATION		
FORM	▪ Title enhances the writing. The thesis of the writing is clear and immediate. Transitions between sections link to the purpose. Each section develops an idea critical to the purpose. The conclusion pulls together all aspects of the writing and clearly links to the thesis.	0 1 2 3 4 5 6
DETAIL	▪ Each idea is fully developed and relates back to the purpose of the writing. Possible questions of the readers are addressed. The writing clearly relates to the figures and graphs presented. Graphs are used to illustrate trends in data.	0 1 2 3 4 5 6
STYLE	▪ The straightforward, clear syntax aids in the audience's understanding. Precise and economical word choice appeals to audience and supports purpose. Ambiguity is avoided. Tone is consistent to purpose. Abstract ideas are carefully explained. Active voice and third person are used.	0 1 2 3 4 5 6
LAYOUT	▪ The layout clarifies the meaning through appropriate headings and labeling that specifically prepare the reader for the upcoming content. Illustrations, diagrams, charts, and/or tables simplify the explanation of complex ideas and are well placed. The layout is consistent as to font, bullets, underlining, and so forth, so that the document presents a unified, coherent impression to the reader.	0 1 2 3 4 5 6
CREATIVITY	▪ Individual insight is expressed in relation to the content.	0 1 2 3 4 5 6
	▪ Individual spark is expressed in relation to the presentation.	0 1 2 3 4 5 6
REFLECTION	▪ Reflection on the learning of the content through product development is apparent.	0 1 2 3 4 5 6
	▪ Reflection on what the student learned about self as a learner is apparent.	0 1 2 3 4 5 6

Comments

_____

_____

Meaning of Performance Scale:

6—PROFESSIONAL LEVEL: level expected from a professional in the content area

5—ADVANCED LEVEL: level exceeds expectations of the standard

4—PROFICIENT LEVEL: level expected for meeting the standard

3—PROGRESSING LEVEL: level demonstrates movement toward the standard

2—NOVICE LEVEL: level demonstrates initial awareness and knowledge of standard

1—NONPERFORMING LEVEL: level indicates no effort made to meet standard

0—NONPARTICIPATING LEVEL: level indicates nothing turned in

Note. Adapted from *Strategies for Differentiating Instruction: Best Practices for the Classroom* (2nd ed.; p. 212), by J. L. Roberts and T. F. Inman, 2007, Waco, TX: Prufrock Press. Copyright © 2007 by Prufrock Press. Adapted with permission.

TECHNICAL REPORT TIER 3—DAP TOOL

CONTENT			
	▪ Content is accurate and thorough in detail.		0 1 2 3 4 5 6
	▪ Product shows complex understanding and manipulation of content.		0 1 2 3 4 5 6
	▪ Product shows deep probing of content.		0 1 2 3 4 5 6
	▪ Organization is best suited to the product.		0 1 2 3 4 5 6
PRESENTATION			
	FORM	▪ Title reflects purpose. The thesis is immediately clear, and the writing is focused. Transitions subtly link all aspects together. Sections fully develop key concepts or ideas critical to the purpose. Conclusion refers back to the purpose of the document and summarizes pertinent knowledge and information. The significance of the conclusion is explained.	0 1 2 3 4 5 6
	DETAIL	▪ Each idea is thoroughly substantiated through pertinent detail or analyzed support. Writing anticipates readers' possible misunderstandings and handles complex ideas clearly. Strong, elaborate support proves points. Only pertinent information is included. The reader is clearly directed to figures and graphs for validation of ideas within the text. How variables were handled is explained.	0 1 2 3 4 5 6
	Style	▪ The straightforward syntax clearly enhances purpose. Diction is precise, economical, and succinct to avoid ambiguity. Tone consistently maintains the audience's attention. Concrete images clarify abstract ideas. Active voice and third person are used skillfully.	0 1 2 3 4 5 6
	LAYOUT	▪ Purposeful manipulation of layout enhances understanding through carefully selected headings. The format is highly consistent as to font, bullets, underlining, and so forth, so that a professional, unified impression is presented to the reader. Illustrations, diagrams, charts, or tables develop and/or explain complex ideas fully. Placement enhances understanding.	0 1 2 3 4 5 6
CREATIVITY		▪ Individual insight is originally expressed in relation to the content.	0 1 2 3 4 5 6
		▪ Individual spark is originally expressed in relation to the presentation.	0 1 2 3 4 5 6
REFLECTION		▪ Insightful reflection on the learning of the content through product development is expressed.	0 1 2 3 4 5 6
		▪ Insightful reflection on what the student learned about self as a learner is expressed.	0 1 2 3 4 5 6

Comments

_____

_____

Meaning of Performance Scale:

6—PROFESSIONAL LEVEL: level expected from a professional in the content area

5—ADVANCED LEVEL: level exceeds expectations of the standard

4—PROFICIENT LEVEL: level expected for meeting the standard

3—PROGRESSING LEVEL: level demonstrates movement toward the standard

2—NOVICE LEVEL: level demonstrates initial awareness and knowledge of standard

1—NONPERFORMING LEVEL: level indicates no effort made to meet standard

0—NONPARTICIPATING LEVEL: level indicates nothing turned in

Note. Adapted from *Strategies for Differentiating Instruction: Best Practices for the Classroom* (2nd ed.; p. 213), by J. L. Roberts and T. F. Inman, 2007, Waco, TX: Prufrock Press. Copyright © 2007 by Prufrock Press. Adapted with permission.

ACTION LESSON 2

Library Wish List

Preparation

Purpose: To provide students with a real-world opportunity to demonstrate how gathering, analyzing, and interpreting data, then using the results to foster a change, can impact the lives of children.

Students Will Understand:
- that a survey can help us gain a better understanding of a group of individuals;
- that, when conducting a survey, there are ethical issues that must be considered such as anonymity, respect, and privacy; and
- that graphs can help make organizing data easier.

Students Will Be Able To:
- assist the librarian with choosing books that they want to read.

Instructional Strategies Used:
- Guided inquiry

Materials Needed:
- Copies of Library Wish List handout

Implementation

Time Needed: 4 weeks

Instructions:
- This action research project is more sophisticated than Action Lesson 1. There are several ways you can choose to do this project: whole class, small groups (each group member is assigned a particular task), or as an extension to high-ability students and others who have shown a particular talent for this topic.

- Once you decide who will work on this project, you want to get students to do a task analysis to determine all of the intermediary steps necessary to carry out and complete the larger project. For example, some intermediary tasks are:
  o Determine how reading levels and Lexile levels are assigned to books and what they mean.
  o Investigate the awards that are given to children's and young adult literature.
  o Find lists of award-winning books.
  o Determine if there are specific rules about what can and cannot be contained in books in our library (e.g., "bad" language, violence).
  o Decide how to survey all students. For example,
    » Will everyone get the entire list of books?
    » Will different grades get a different set of books (e.g., kindergarten gets a list of 15 books with reading levels from K–3, whereas fourth grade might get books from grades 3–7)?
    » Will surveys for primary students look different than those for upper elementary?
    » How will you have students who can't read take the survey?

  o Decide whether to assign different tasks to different people or work on everything together.

- We advise having students create a list of no more than 100 books to use in their serveys. After students have been surveyed, we suggest you have your class narrow down their original list to include those found to be most desirable to survey respondents.
- You might want to check with your local public library or university to see if there is a children's literature specialist who could come and talk to your students about selecting books.

LIBRARY WISH LIST

Our school library has just received a grant of $2,000 to purchase new books for the library! Our librarian heard that we were studying about how to conduct surveys, and she wants our help. She would like us to determine what books students at our school would like to have in the library. She has provided the following guidelines based on the terms of the grant.

The books selected must:

- span reading levels from K–12,
- include both male and female main characters,
- reflect diversity,
- be award-winning literature, and
- include both fiction and nonfiction selections.

In a spreadsheet, our librarian would like the following from each book: its title, author, a brief (2–3 sentences) description, and price. She has given us a month to present our final list of books to her. I hope you will decide to take on this task.

Unit 2
Experimental Research

This unit is designed to teach students the process of doing experimental research.

What You Will Find in This Unit

PRETEACHING LESSON

What Are Experiments?

Preparation

Purpose: To understand experimental research.

Students Will Know:

- **Experiment** (noun): A way to find out about some natural world phenomenon through an investigation.
- **Process** (noun): A method or procedure.
- **Evidence** (noun or verb): That which proves or disproves something (noun); to offer proof of something (verb).
- **Hypothesis** (noun): A preconception of what one hopes to verify in the experiment.
- **Linear** (adjective): Sequential; based on a series of steps to get to an end result.
- **Cycle** (noun): A depiction of a series of events or operations that are related in some way and usually lead back to the starting point.

Students Will Understand:

- that experimentation involves testing ideas about the natural world with data gathered from it;
- that the experimental process is nonlinear;
- that, when we undertake the experimental process, we use observation, exploration, testing, communication, and other science process skills;
- that the How Science Works flowchart helps us understand how to conduct experimental investigations; and
- that an individual can be an agent of change by designing an experiment to test a particular hypothesis that could provide information to support a reason for policy makers to effect a change.

Students Will Be Able To:

- follow the process of science through the simple flowchart when given an example of an investigation, and
- diagram the flow of an investigation through the complex flowchart.

Instructional Strategies Used:
- Guided inquiry
- Graphic organizer
- Exit cards

Materials Needed:
- Copies of Graphic Organizer handout
- Copies of Exit Card handout
- Copies of the How Science Works simple and complex flowcharts found at http://undsci.berkeley.edu
    - This website provides excellent information about the nature and process of science, including the How Science Works flowchart used in this unit. There are many useful teacher-friendly activities by grade band as well as other resource material (select How Science Works, then Next). The How Science Works simple and complex flowcharts can be accessed directly at http://undsci.berkeley.edu/teaching/teachingtools.php

- Copies of books for students to use. Several are listed in the lesson, but other similar books can be used. It is best to have a book for each student if possible. The entire class does not need to have the same book.

Implementation

Time Needed: Varies

Instructions:
- Introduce students to the How Science Works flowchart. You can make copies of both the simple and complex forms for students to reference, but having them access the interactive version of the chart online (http://undsci.berkeley.edu/article/scienceflowchart) on their laptops would be most effective. If students don't have laptops or other such devices, demonstrate the interactive nature on the SMART Board. The How Science Works flowchart is critical to a clear understanding of the process of scientific investigation. In many cases, students have been exposed to a step-by-step linear process, which has been reinforced by colorful classroom posters depicting these steps. Students often get the impression that the process is like following a recipe in a cookbook, rather than a cyclical process.
- Explain the terminology found on the flowchart. Make sure students understand the concepts of *Benefits and Outcomes* and *Community*

Analysis and Feedback as well as all of the subheadings found on the interactive chart (which appear upon hovering the cursor over a category; note that these are the same categories that appear in the complex version of the flowchart). Once students have a good understanding of the parts of the flowchart, proceed to the next part of the lesson.

- When ready, have students select one of the following books:
  o *Rocks in His Head* by Carol Otis Hurst
  o *Snowflake Bentley* by Jacqueline Briggs Martin
  o *The Fossil Girl* by Catherine Brighton
  o *Dive: My Adventures in the Deep Frontier* by Sylvia A. Earle
  o *Marie Curie* by Leonard Everett Fisher
  o *Gifted Hands: The Ben Carson Story* by Benjamin S. Carson
  o *Madame C. J. Walker & New Cosmetics* by Katherine Krohn
  o *Luis Walker Álvarez* by Tina Randall

  If a student prefers a book of his or her own choosing, please be sure that it describes a scientific investigation.

- Have students read their chosen books. Next, provide each student with the Graphic Organizer worksheet. Explain that students should find evidence about how their scientists followed the flowchart they have been studying. Have them place the evidence on the graphic organizer. Once all organizers are completed, engage students in a discussion about their evidence. Have them find similarities and differences among the different scientists' approaches. Have them pay particular attention to the bottom two quadrants of the graphic organizer. Perhaps making a list of all of the contributions of the various scientists and a discussion about how they have affected our lives would be helpful.

- Once you are sure that students have a good understanding of the flowchart and how it is used in scientific investigations, have students complete the Exit Card. The information from the card will assist you in determining who might need some reeaching and who has an excellent understanding of the concepts.

Differentiation

- You may differentiate for students who have difficulty comprehending complex information by having them work solely with the simple How Science Works flowchart during Step 1 of Implementation.
- The Teaching Tools section of the Understanding Science website will provide you with developmentally appropriate activities and suggestions for reinforcing the concepts in the flowchart should you need them. It

can be accessed at http://undsci.berkeley.edu/teaching/teachingtools.
php.

- The book list may be differentiated by having a selection of books that match the reading levels of your students.

Name:_____ Date: _____

GRAPHIC ORGANIZER

Name of Scientist:_____

Exploration and Discovery	Testing Ideas
Benefits and Outcomes	**Community Analysis and Feedback**

XIT CARD

Works flowchart. Add as much detail as you can.

95

Control and Experimental Groups

Preparation

Purpose: To understand the need for control and experimental groups in investigations.

Students Will Know:

- **Control group** (noun): In an investigation, the variable or variables under investigation are not changed.
- **Experimental group** (noun): The group that receives the experimental condition; it is exposed to the independent variable.
- **Variable** (noun): In an investigation, any factor that can be controlled or changed.
- **Independent variable** (noun): The condition that you change in an experiment.
- **Dependent variable** (noun): The variable in which the independent variable causes a change.

Students Will Understand:

- that an independent variable causes a change in a dependent variable, but a dependent variable cannot cause a change in an independent variable;
- that investigations need to have all variables except one independent variable controlled in the experimental group to determine if the changes in the independent variable cause a change in the dependent variable;
- that changing more than one variable at a time does not allow the investigator to determine which variable caused the change; and
- that the How Science Works flowchart helps us understand how to conduct experimental investigations.

Students Will Be Able To:

- use the vocabulary appropriately,

- distinguish between independent and dependent variables in an investigation, and
- determine if an experiment has been properly controlled.

Instructional Strategies Used:
- Case studies/scenarios

Materials Needed:
- Scenarios
- Copies of Experimental Design 1 handout
- Copies of Experimental Design 2 handout

Implementation

Time Needed: Varies

Instructions:
- Use a SMART Board or other device to project the following so that all students can see it:

    Mr. Cortez's class has been studying friction and wanted to design an investigation to test their idea that objects will travel faster on a smooth surface than on a rough surface. The students gathered several different surfaces: a smooth piece of countertop material, fine sandpaper, coarse sandpaper, carpet, and a piece of wood paneling. They cut all pieces of material to fit on a triangular sloping platform that measured 12 inches high, 16 inches long at the base, and 20 inches on the hypotenuse. They used a stopwatch to measure the time it took the same small nonelectric car to travel down the slope with each different type of material. The students gathered the data and determined that the smoother the surface, the faster the car traveled.

- Ask students to determine the independent variable (surfaces with various degrees of friction) and the dependent variable (speed). Ask: *What was controlled in the experiment?* (Type of car, platform, size of materials) *What was the experimental condition?* (Change in type of material)
- Then, project this scenario:

    Sara, Martin, and Jade each decided independently to try the same experiment at home. Sara designed her experiment exactly like the one at school except that her platform was 6" x 8" x 10". Martin borrowed the platform from school and used the same materials, but because he had a large collection of small cars, he used a different kind for each material.

EXPERIMENTAL DESIGN 2

Directions: Pretend you were going to set up experiments to answer each question below. Identify the experimental and control group in each one.

What is the effect of light on plant growth?

What amount of light will attract moths?

Does the amount of air affect the time a candle burns?

What is the effect of pressure on the shape of a marshmallow?

At what distance will a magnet continue to attract?

- Have students go back to the Experimental Design 1 worksheet from the previous lesson and focus on the question they chose to investigate. Have students make a list of the possible ethical issues that might arise and explain how they will address them. If they need assistance, refer them to the "Ethics in Research" website (see the Materials Needed list). Have students revisit the Frayer Model to add additional information based on the discussions during this lesson.

FRAYER MODEL: ETHICS

Definition	Characteristics

Ethics

Examples	Nonexamples

LESSON 3

How Do They Know That?

Preparation

Purpose: To understand how to determine whether the evidence from investigations supports the claims being made.

Students Will Know:
- **Claim** (noun or verb): An assertion of something as a fact (noun); to make such an assertion (verb).
- **Evidence** (noun or verb): That which proves or disproves something (noun); to offer proof of something (verb).

Students Will Understand:
- that advertisements in the media make claims about products or services to get consumers to buy their goods or services;
- that some consumers purchase these goods or services based on whether or not they believe the claim and others purchase the items based on other factors such as whether they like the celebrity who is promoting the product;
- that few consumers dig deeper to find the research evidence that supports the claim; and
- that the How Science Works flowchart helps us understand how to conduct experimental investigations.

Students Will Be Able To:
- use the vocabulary appropriately, and
- determine the validity of the claims made by a manufacturer by looking at the evidence.

Instructional Strategies Used:
- Video
- Discussion
- Frayer Model

Materials Needed:
- "Energizer vs. Duracell: Which Battery Packs the Most Energy?" (http://voices.yahoo.com/energizer-vs-duracell-which-battery-packs-most-347548.html)
- "Energizer E2 Vs. Rayovac Rechargeable Batteries" (http://voices.yahoo.com/energizer-e2-vs-rayovac-rechargable-batteries-32458.html?cat=15)
- Three YouTube videos (*Note:* check for suitability before using):
  o "Advertiser vs. Consumer" (http://www.youtube.com/watch?v=heSudg-tfIk)
  o "Psychology and Advertising" (http://www.youtube.com/watch?v=EC7VLjIw8hY&feature=related)
  o "Where Good Ideas Come From" (http://www.youtube.com/watch?v=NugRZGDbPFU&feature=related)

- A subscription to *Consumer Reports*, if possible (if not, purchase a few issues at a magazine stand)
- Newspapers and/or magazines

Implementation

Time Needed: Varies

Instructions:
- Begin by asking students if they know any claims made by advertisers. If they aren't sure, prompt them with one they have probably heard, such as *Nine out of 10 dentists recommend Colgate toothpaste.* Ask them how the advertiser knows the information in the claim is true. Students may suggest that they called and asked 10 dentists, and nine said yes. Preview the three YouTube videos listed in the Materials Needed section for appropriateness, and then use those that you deem appropriate to give students additional perspectives on advertising claims.
- Based on what they have learned so far, ask the students how they would set up an investigation to test a claim. Write the suggestions on chart paper or the SMART Board so that everyone can see. Prompt students when necessary to be sure they are not missing any steps. Ask students how they could find out how the advertiser conducted the investigation to make the claim.
- Ask students how many of them have battery-operated devices. Ask them to name the batteries they use. Write down all that are named. Ask students how they choose (or would choose) the battery they use (e.g., they like the Energizer bunny, that a particular commercial about

using the battery in a toy was good). Here are two versions of battery testing investigations: http://voices.yahoo.com/energizer-vs-duracell-which-battery-packs-most-347548.html and http://voices.yahoo.com/energizer-e2-vs-rayovac-rechargable-batteries-32458.html?cat=15. Both offer experiments to determine which battery is superior over at least one other battery. Make copies and give half of the students one investigation and half the other. Have them look for the parts of an experiment that they have studied thus far. Have them also refer to the How Science Works flowchart to determine what areas are and are not represented in the investigations. Ask each group to explain the evidence that was presented and, based on the evidence, which battery they would pick now.

- Have students watch infomercials, read articles in *Consumer Reports*, bring in examples of advertising claims found in newspapers or magazines, or copy down claims they hear in commercials on television, YouTube, and the radio. They can also take screenshots of pop-up advertising on the web. Once you have a collection of claims, have students assist you in designing a template that can be used to gather evidence to determine if the claim can be supported or must be refuted. Have students determine how best to present the information they have gathered and demonstrate what they learned to a real-world audience, such as the Better Business Bureau, Angie's List, or other similar organizations. They might consider sharing what they found with manufacturers if they found different results than what was claimed in the manufacturers' advertisements. If a manufacturer or advertiser responds, or materials are revised based on the students' research, be sure students understand how their actions made a difference.

- Have students look again at the How Science Works flowchart. Engage students in a discussion about how we know certain claims are true or not.

Differentiation

- For students who are interested in studying how advertisers gain the information they need to make their claims, provide support for necessary resources, such as phone calls, how to write a business letter, searching the Internet, and so forth.

ACTION LESSON 1

Keep It Growing!

Preparation

Purpose: To understand how to complete a controlled experiment.

Students Will Understand:
- that investigations need to have all variables, except one independent variable, controlled in the experimental group to determine if the changes in the independent variable cause a change in the dependent variable, and
- that the How Science Works flowchart helps us understand how to conduct experimental investigations.

Students Will Be Able To:
- determine the optimum conditions for growing vegetables in a garden.

Instructional Strategies Used:
- Guided inquiry
- Discussion

Materials Needed:
- Garden tools (e.g., hoes, trowels)
- Seed catalogs
- Seeds (based on student choice)
- Small flower pots
- Potting soil
- Paper towels
- Measuring cups

Implementation

Note to Teachers:

This action research project is designed so that students ultimately plant an actual vegetable garden whose bounty could be divided among the children to take home, provide fresh vegetables for the school cafeteria, provide fresh vegetables for a food pantry, or for some other use decided upon by the students. But before students can begin to develop a garden, they must first perform a series of controlled experiments to determine the optimum conditions that will provide the best yield of each crop. Contacting the local extension office and/or having a local master gardener come and speak to the class will give the class opportunities to ask questions of people who have expertise growing crops locally. The Urban Harvest Community Gardens Program has an informative website that may be of help; it can be accessed at http://www.urbanharvest.org/cgardens/startguide.html.

To assist with the initial costs, seek grants from community foundations or your school parent organization, or consider unique ways that students can raise the money themselves. Be sure to document and publicize your project; having this documentation may assist you in garnering more funds if you chose to repeat the project with another group of students. Photos are always a great way to document progress.

Time Needed: several months (all parts)

Instructions:

Part 1

- Check with school officials for permission to use an area of the school grounds.
- Contact the local extension agent, master gardening group, or horticulture department of a nearby college or university to get ideas about crops that grow well in your area as well as input about the best place for the garden. Be sure to test the soil at this time.
- Research the pros and cons of making an organic garden and determine how you will control pests.
- Gather seed catalogs or take a field trip to a gardening center to purchase seeds and other necessary items (small flowerpots, soil, etc.). Remember, right now you are just going to perform a series of controlled experiments to determine optimum growth conditions.
- You may choose a variety of ways to set up the experiments. For example, divide the students into groups of 2–3 and have each group responsible for one crop. For example, there can be a radish group, a carrot group, a tomato group, a pumpkin group, a bell pepper group, and so forth.

- Have all necessary materials available in a central location, including measuring cups, trowels, paper towels, etc.
- Have each group develop their experimental design in a science journal kept for the purpose of the garden project. Meet with each group individually to discuss their designs before allowing them to collect their materials. Be sure students have a control plant as well as experimental plants. Be sure they are using the How Science Works flowchart to assist in their designs.
- Once a group's design has been approved, allow them to collect their materials and proceed with setting up the experiments.
- It will take several weeks to complete the experimental phase of the project. Be sure to allow time each day for students to collect data, write notes in their journals, and draw pictures/diagrams of each stage as plants begin to grow. Be sure they can recognize when their chosen crop is ripe.
- Conference weekly with individual groups while observing all students daily.
- Once all experiments have been completed, data analyzed, and results and conclusions discussed, have each group make recommendations for the garden based on their results.

Part 2

- Enlist help from parents, community members, faculty, other students, and anyone else who might want to help in preparing the garden. The *For Dummies* website provides good directions for preparing a garden; they can be accessed at http://www.dummies.com/how-to/content/how-to-prepare-garden-soil-for-planting.html. (*Note:* This phase can occur concurrently with the experimentation process. That way, the garden is ready when students have their recommendations based on the results of their experiments.)
- Once the garden is prepared, begin planting. Be sure to make labels so you know which crop is planted where.
- Based on the crops you chose and your particular climate, be sure to have a plan developed for caring for the garden. What will you do if there isn't enough rain? What about weeds? What about wildlife that think you planted the garden for its use? How often will you check on the garden? What about weekends? What about school holidays?
- Decide how to distribute the bounty based on the choices students made at the beginning of the project.

Differentiation

- Interested students can continue with other projects based on their work. Some examples might be creating recipes that use their crops, starting a food pantry for the school, or sharing their work with other schools that have completed similar projects.

ACTION LESSON 2

The Power of Preservatives

Preparation

Purpose: To learn about different preservatives and their effect on molds and bacteria that can spoil food.

Students Will Understand:

- that preservatives work to keep food fresh;
- that mold can form on different foods and general information regarding how and why;
- that safety procedures must be kept in place for both the investigators and the object of the investigation (and the implications of what could happen if safety procedures are violated); and
- that the How Science Works flowchart helps us understand how to conduct experimental investigations.

Students Will Be Able To:

- perform controlled experiments involving mold growth on foods that do and do not contain preservatives.

Instructional Strategies Used:

- Guided inquiry
- Discussion

Materials Needed:

- Goggles
- Plastic, latex, or nonlatex gloves
- Chart paper
- Markers
- Clear plastic containers with colored lids
- copies of KWHL Chart for Mold handout
- copies of KWHL Chart for Preservatives handout
- copies of Preservatives Chart handout

Implementation

Note to Teachers:

Do not use meats or fish in this activity. It will be important for students to understand the safety precautions needed for this project. Goggles and plastic gloves will be necessary. If you use latex gloves, check with parents to be sure students are not allergic to latex, or find a source for nonlatex gloves.

Time Needed: 2–4 weeks (depending on the investigations)

Instructions:

- Ask students about any experiences they have had with moldy food. Have they seen mold on food or accidentally started to eat a piece of food and then noticed the mold? Are there instances where mold on food is good? Is mold a plant or an animal? (It is neither!) What is it? To what kingdom does it belong? What are its characteristics? Use a KWHL chart (*Know, Want to Know, How Will I Find Information, What I Learned*) to gather information on mold. You can make this on chart paper, project it on a SMART Board, or have individual charts for students to complete (see the KWHL Chart for Mold handout). Once students have completed their research on molds, have them do similar research on preservatives. What are common preservatives? What were some preservatives used in earlier times? Are there problems associated with preservatives? What foods generally contain preservatives? Use the KWHL Chart for Preservatives to gather information.

- Next, have students choose a meal and complete the Preservatives Chart. Have students bring their completed charts to class and discuss the results. Have students determine the percentage of preserved food versus nonpreserved food that they ate. What was the average amount of food eaten with preservatives? Which students ate the least amount of preserved food? Looking at all of their data, did a particular meal (breakfast, lunch, dinner) seem to have more preserved foods than others?

- Now that students have some understanding of molds and preservatives, have them formulate questions that they would like to answer through controlled experiments. Here are some examples that you might expect:
  o What foods are good substrates (bases) for growing mold?
  o Do fresh foods mold faster than foods with preservatives?
  o Can mold growth be retarded in fresh foods that have no preservatives?

- Students with the same questions can work together, although groups should be no larger than four students (larger groups seem to work less efficiently). Have students design their controlled experiments and submit them for approval before they begin. Because all students will be working with mold, you need to take precautions that the mold spores will not be accidentally released into the air once they have grown on the food. Here are nonnegotiables for these experiments:

o Students need to use goggles and gloves.

o Although some activities available on the Internet or in books may suggest glass containers, to use them runs the risk of breakage and the release of molds into the air. If you do decide to use glass containers, baby food or jelly jars work well, but clear plastic containers are safer.

o To get a close look at the molds when using a container with a colored lid, put the food on the lid portion and set the container over the lid (your container will be upside down). Then you can see the mold through the clear container situated on top.

o *Regardless of the container, once the food is in the container, seal the lid with tape and never open it again!*

▪ Once students have completed their experiments, have them present their results to each other. Have students review their KWHL charts and complete them based on the results of their research and experiments.

o There are several ways students can effect a change as a result of completing their research and experimentation. Here are some examples:

o Write a persuasive letter to the school dietician arguing for food with fewer preservatives, citing facts from their research and experimentation.

o Persuade parents to lessen the amount of food with preservatives that is brought into the home. Make a list of favorite foods and find versions without preservatives, or search for recipes to make them from scratch. For example, a student who loves spaghetti could determine how to make the sauce with no preservatives.

o Hold a research symposium on molds and preservatives. Consider inviting individuals who would be interested in mold growth and preservatives (e.g., lunchroom personnel, dieticians, science personnel from local colleges/universities, family members).

Differentiation

▪ Allow interested students to pursue any topics of interest that they would like to explore after the discussions.

- You may choose to differentiate the experiments based on student readiness to conduct an investigation. If so, you should assign the following resources to the appropriate groups.
  - o For a simple experiment, students can use the Mold Terrarium activity at the Exploratorium website (http://www.exploratorium.edu/science_explorer/mold.html).
  - o For more complex experiments, students can use either The Effect of Environmental Factors on Mold Growth (http://www.mthsscience.org/Science_fair/SF_Biology/Mold%20Growth.pdf) or Mold Bread Experiment (http://www.experiment-resources.com/mold-bread-experiment.html).
  - o For experiments that involve mold and preservatives, students can visit Food Preservation: Science Fair Projects and Experiments (http://www.juliantrubin.com/fairprojects/food/food_preservation.html).

Name: _____ Date: _____

KWHL CHART FOR MOLD

What I Know	What I Want to Know	How Can I Find Out	What I Learned

Name:_____ Date:_____

KWHL CHART FOR PRESERVATIVES

What I Know	What I Want to Know	How Can I Find Out	What I Learned

Name:_____Date: _____

PRESERVATIVES CHART

Meal: _____

Directions: Complete the chart by entering the information about each type of food you ate. Include sauces, condiments, and anything else you might have added to the food. For example, if you ate green beans and added butter, list both the beans and the butter. Be sure you let the person preparing the food know that you need information about the food before he or she puts food containers in the trash. You will have to look at the ingredient list on packaged foods to determine what preservatives were used. For the Form column, list if the item was in a can, box, package, frozen, or fresh.

Name of Food	Form	Contains Preservative(s)	Name of Preservative(s)

Section 4
Qualitative Research

Unit 3
Life History

This unit is designed to teach students the process of doing life history research.

What You Will Find in This Unit

What Are Life Histories?

Preparation

Purpose: To understand life histories and life history research.

Students Will Know:
- **Life History** (noun): "The story a person chooses to tell about the life he or she has lived, told as completely and honestly as possible, what is remembered of it, and what the teller wants others to know of it, usually as a result of a guided interview by another" and "a fairly complete narrating of one's entire experience of life as a whole, highlighting the most important aspects" (Atkinson, 1998, p. 8).

Students Will Understand:
- life histories as well as life history research and its utility as action research.

Students Will Be Able To:
- articulate the definition of a life history;
- collect life history data through the use of the following methods: interview conversations, group work, timelines, personal writing (e.g., journals, diaries), and documents (Goodson & Sikes, 2001); and
- understand the utility of life history as action research.

Instructional Strategies Used:
- Guided inquiry
- Brainstorming
- Case studies

Materials Needed:
- Copies of Life History Research Pyramid handout
- Copies of The Public Library Creative Commons case study handout (if needed)
- Copies of Life History Choice Board handout

Implementation

Time Needed: 60 minutes

Instructions:

- Start by asking the students to complete the Life History Research Pyramid worksheet. Encourage students to attempt to reach the goals put forward on the worksheet. Once the students have completed the worksheets individually, or after a set period of time (approximately 3–5 minutes), ask for a few volunteers to assist you in creating a comprehensive list of keywords, methods, and people based on input from the class members. You can use a whiteboard, chalkboard, flip chart, SMART Board, or even a wiki to create three lists for the whole class to view.

- As you are eliciting the keywords, methods, and people from the whole group, ask the students who volunteer items from their worksheet to explain their rationale for their selections. For example, if a student suggests "newspaper" as a keyword, ask what he or she was thinking when the word was written. Newspapers can be excellent sources of life history data because they chronicle the events of an area over time and can include significant events such as graduations, weddings, and obituaries. Newspapers are "time-stamped," so they offer much contextual information to researchers engaged in life history research.

- Once the comprehensive lists are created, ask the students to offer a definition of life history research. In what ways can they make use of the keywords to articulate a definition? Offer them the definition put forward by Atkinson (1998).

- Next, talk the students through the means of data collection within the master list. Spend time on data sources that may seem less obvious such as timelines or documents. Timelines may be helpful tools for subjects of life history projects to complete as they narrate their lives within interviews and/or oral histories. Documents such as deeds, newspapers, birth certificates, and letters can be helpful in piecing together life histories.

- Ask the students to consider the individuals they listed on the bottom of the pyramid. Why are they interested in these lives? How might the stories of these individuals' lives impact action or change? What types of research questions would lead to a life history project? Finally, if necessary, you can use the example case study (The Public Library Creative Commons) to assist in your facilitation of this line of questioning within the lesson. You can work through this case as a whole class or divide your students into groups to brainstorm responses to the questions posed.

Differentiation

- Provide each student with the Life History Choice Board worksheet, which is based on life history research.
- Ask each student to complete three of the choices on the board using the concept of tic-tac-toe. Students must choose a "winning" combination. Please note that some of the choices require students to use websites for which you will need to set up a school account first to ensure their safety and privacy.
- Either collect students' work, ask them to present their work to the class or in small groups, or ask them to complete the work as an anchoring activity.
- Students' work can be used simply as an activity or for a grade.

Name:_____ Date: _____

LIFE HISTORY RESEARCH PYRAMID

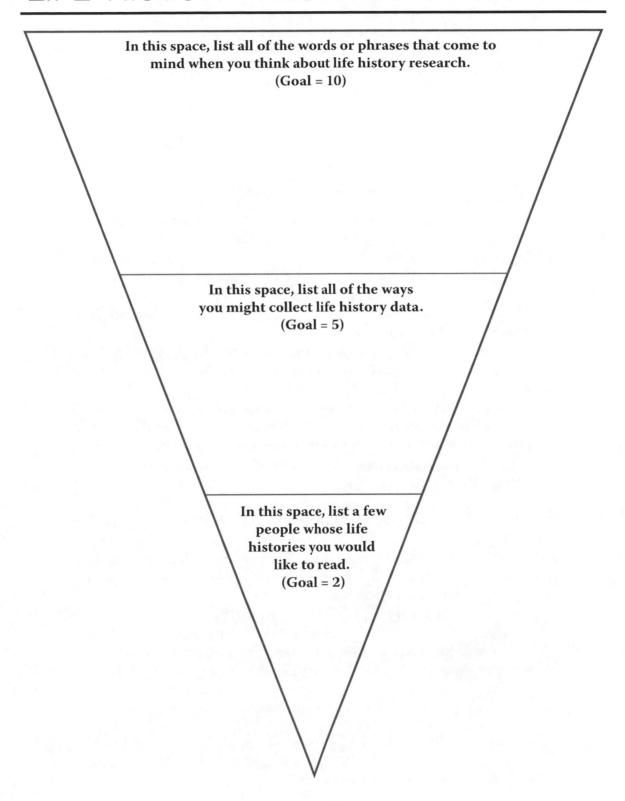

In this space, list all of the words or phrases that come to mind when you think about life history research.
(Goal = 10)

In this space, list all of the ways you might collect life history data.
(Goal = 5)

In this space, list a few people whose life histories you would like to read.
(Goal = 2)

A PARTNERSHIP BETWEEN LIFE HISTORY AND ACTION RESEARCH

The Public Library Creative Commons

Your local public library has recently administered a survey to its members in an attempt to better understand library patrons' needs and the new ways in which an underutilized room in the library might be repurposed to bolster utilization. The results of the survey indicated the following:

1. The library patrons are interested in a destination space within the library dedicated to creative projects such as sewing, beading, model building (e.g., planes, trains, rockets), collage, crochet, and whittling.

2. Because of low participation across the middle schools within the geopolitical region the library serves, a countywide LEGO robotics team has been formed. The team consistently struggles to find a place to build, and team numbers have been low. The survey indicated that patrons would like to dedicate the space to team practices.

3. Three women founded the library in the mid-1960s. The library is positioned in a part of town that has historically been the division between "white" and "black" sections of town, and the racial divides are still visible. The women who founded the library, all of whom were teachers within the area at the time, thought of the building as a symbolic bridge between the two communities, a place for understanding, reconciliation, and cultural learning. The library patrons expressed an interest in honoring these three women through the space in some way.

You and your research team have been contracted to conduct further research in response to the question, *How should the library's space be repurposed?* In response to this charge, you decide to conduct life history research on these three women. Only two of the three women are still alive today, and one of those two currently lives in another state.

Consider the following:

- Within this case, details are missing. What are the needed details? What do you need to know before conducting the life history research?
- What difference would it make if this public library were located in your actual town or a town in some other state? Which other state?
- In what ways might the life history research impact your proposed plans for the space in the library?
- What might you find in the process of completing this research?
- How might this process play out in the end? (Use your imagination!)
- How might this life history project be seen as a form of action research?

Name:_____   Date: _____

LIFE HISTORY CHOICE BOARD

Visit and explore this website: http://www.sussex.ac.uk/clhlwr. Compose an e-mail to the director that includes your questions about life history, things you would like to know about the center, and any questions you might have about the university.	Imagine you have just received a contract to write a book entitled: *Mythical Life Histories: How Modern Superheroes Came to Be.* How would you go about doing the research for this book? Which superheroes would you select to include (e.g., Superman, Catwoman, Green Lantern, Iron Man, Wonder Woman, Thor). What would your book look like? Create a presentation on this endeavor using PowerPoint, Prezi, or Keynote.	Visit and explore this website: http://usm.maine.edu/olli/national/lifestorycenter. You are preparing to visit the Life Story Commons to interview the director, Robert Atkinson. Write up a list of 10 interview questions you would like to ask about life stories and how life stories are alike or different from life history research.
Imagine you are 100 years old! How might your life history look? What do you hope your life history contains? Who ought to write your life history? Compose a letter to your 100-year-old self that explains the details you hope to one day "see" in your life history.	Create an animated short using the websites http://www.xtranormal.com or http://goanimate.com that features two characters: one that represents life history research and one that represents action research. Do these characters get along? Why or why not? What do they have in common? How are they different?	Using the website http://www.pixton.com, create a short comic based on what you now know about life history research. Be as creative as possible!
The local historical society in your area has recently decided to add a junior chapter. They are in the process of creating a book on the history of the schools within the county, and they would like to get young people who have a passion for history involved. You have a passion for history! You join the local junior historical society and are paired up with a senior mentor who has been a part of the society for 12 years. You and your mentor are in charge of crafting a life history research plan for the school history book. What will your plan include? Create an outline, concept map, or drawing to illustrate the plan.	Seek out a copy of your local newspaper. Read through the paper in an attempt to identify content that might be helpful in the composition of a life history project. Create a table with the following column headings: (1) Article Name, (2) Page, (3) Person (Subject of Life History), and (4) Rationale (Why Useful in Life History Research). Fill in the table, and try to scan the entire paper. This can be done online, too—just replace "Page" with "URL."	Conduct an online search for examples of timelines. What do you like about them? What do you dislike? Imagine you are asked to create a handout of "timeline-creating rules" within the context of carrying out life history research. Using these examples as guides, compose the handout for your classmates. Think about what makes a timeline easy to use, appealing, and helpful.

LESSON 1

The People of Our Area

Preparation

Purpose: To identify prominent figures within the geopolitical area in which your school is situated.

Students Will Know:
- **Local History** (noun): The study of the history of a specific geographic area with a focus on the local community.
- **Genealogy** (noun): The study of family histories and lineages.
- **Oral History** (noun): The study and collection of verbal accounts of persons' lives, families, and important events using audio or video records.
- **Archives** (noun): Historical records—including but not limited to photographs, films, letters, diaries, and newspaper articles—of individuals, groups, and institutions that contain information of enduring value.

Students Will Understand:
- how to identify prominent figures within the geopolitical area in which their school is situated.

Students Will Be Able To:
- identify prominent figures within the geopolitical area in which their school is situated.

Instructional Strategies Used:
- Guided inquiry
- Web searching
- Wiki or blog creation
- Field trip

Materials Needed:
- Paper for concept maps
- Copies of Prominent Individuals handout
- Copies of Voter Cards handout

- *The Other Side of Middletown: Exploring Muncie's African American Community* by Luke Eric Lassiter (you may want to locate this through your local library in advance, as it may be difficult to obtain)
- Computers with Internet access

Implementation

Time Needed: Varies

Instructions:
- Start by asking the students to think about the following key terms: *local history*, *genealogy*, *oral history*, and *archives*. Explain to the students that the goal of this lesson is to identify prominent individuals within their local community. Eventually, these individuals will be asked to participate in the students' life history research projects. To identify current prominent individuals within the community, it is important to have an understanding of the community's history and prominent individuals of the past.
- Refer students back to the four terms articulated above. What are these terms, and how might these terms help students reach the goal of the lesson? Guide the students through a brief discussion on these questions.
- Once a basic level of understanding of the terms has been established, divide the class into four groups. Assign each group to one of the terms. Each group will conduct a thorough web scavenger hunt in an attempt to learn as much as possible about these terms. Groups will also want to gather examples of each of the terms—as many as they can. Ask each group to establish a wiki (e.g., http://www.wikispaces.com, http://www.wikidot.com) or blog (e.g., http://wordpress.com, https://www.tumblr.com) to which they will post information gathered from their searches. (You may want to visit these sites and create school/teacher accounts first.)
- At this point, it may be helpful to articulate the final intended outcome of this unit on life history research: to create a website that houses life history research projects conducted by students with prominent individuals within their local community. However, before the creation of the site, preliminary research must be conducted. The creation of the wikis and blogs will serve as foundational content for their final site.
- Ask a representative from each group to share its blog or wiki URL with the whole class. In addition, ask each group to provide a very brief overview (less than 5 minutes) of the results of their web searches.

- Once all students have had the opportunity to review the blogs and/ or wikis, ask each student to draw out a concept map that outlines the process through which they would go to identify prominent individuals within their community. Explain the following parameters for the concept map: (a) a minimum of two of the four featured terms from above must be included in the concept map, and (b) each student must articulate a local field trip that will facilitate the identification process. If students are stumped regarding the field trip, suggest some destinations or ask other students to suggest some destinations. Examples may be the local library, a courthouse, or a local history museum.

- Ask students to get back into their four groups and discuss their proposed field trips. Challenge the groups to come to a consensus on a field trip destination.

- Have each group present their destinations to the whole class and articulate what would take place during the field trip. In other words, how would the field trip allow the class to identify prominent individuals within their local community? For example, will they search archival data, speak with local public servants, or examine court documents?

- Once four viable field trip options have been identified and articulated, ask members of the class to vote on where they would like to go. Rank order the trips in the event that one or more of the options are not possible. Once a top choice is established, engage the students in the planning process for the trip.

- If possible, actually take the field trip and allow the students to plan for their trip activities so as to move closer to the identification of prominent individuals in their community. What exactly will they do on the trip? With whom do they wish to speak? What is the goal of the trip?

- Once the students have returned from the field trip, ask them to break up into their four groups. Each group will complete the Prominent Individuals worksheet. It should be noted here that each person listed on the worksheet must be living and able to provide life history data.

- Each group will make their case for why they selected each individual. Then, each member of the class will vote on the individuals on whom they would like to conduct their life history research. Each student will vote for six individuals by cutting out and completing the voting cards from the Voter Cards worksheet.

- The top six vote-getting individuals will be asked to participate in the life history project to be conducted by the class.

Differentiation

- Within local history research, oftentimes the voices or histories of some groups are silenced. Typically, these voices or histories are of marginalized people within the geopolitical area.
- Encourage the students to use the web to explore the historic Middletown studies.
- Ask them to create a PowerPoint, Prezi, or Keynote presentation that provides an overview of the Middletown studies.
- Then, expose the students to the book *The Other Side of Middletown: Exploring Muncie's African American Community* by Luke Eric Lassiter. A DVD is also available. What was the purpose of this book? How was the project undertaken? What was uncovered in the process?
- How might the students be certain that *all* voices are represented within their life history research?
- Ask students to devise a plan to ensure representation of all peoples and places within the geopolitical area in which their school is situated.
- The plan can take the form of an outline, checklist, or any other viable format the students devise.

Name:_____Date: _____

PROMINENT INDIVIDUALS

Directions: In the small boxes, list the names of individuals on whom your group would like to conduct life history research. List them in rank order (i.e., 1 = highest interest, 4 = lowest interest). In the space below each name, provide a rationale for why you have selected each person.

1.	2.
3.	4.

VOTER CARDS

Directions: Complete the voter cards below. Cut the paper into six strips and place the strips into the ballot box. You may only vote for six individuals. You may not vote for one individual more than once.

Your Name:	Vote:

Your Name:	Vote:

Your Name:	Vote:

Your Name:	Vote:

Your Name:	Vote:

Your Name:	Vote:

LESSON 2

Interviewing

Preparation

Purpose: To understand the interview process.

Students Will Know:
- **Open-ended** (adjective): A type of question that allows responders to provide any answer they choose.
- **Closed** (adjective): A type of question that requires responders to choose an answer from several choices.

Students Will Understand:
- the interview process, and
- the difference between closed and open-ended questions.

Students Will Be Able To:
- conduct an interview.

Instructional Strategies Used:
- Group work
- Trial and error
- Group interviewing
- RAFT (role, audience, format, topic)

Materials Needed:
- List of suggested interview questions
- Notepad
- Digital voice recorders
- Copies of Interviewing handout

Implementation

Time Needed: Varies

Instructions:
Part 1

- Some prior planning is necessary for the implementation of this lesson. A few weeks ahead of implementation, solicit the participation of a few individuals who are willing to be interviewed by your students. Ask for student input. About whom would they like to know more? Some examples might be high school seniors, members of a local athletic team, firefighters, local business owners, or community volunteers.
- Ask the individuals to join you for the session when you plan to implement the lesson.
- As you prepare for their visit, provide the students with background information on the individuals. What would they like to know? How might they ask questions to allow them to garner this information?
- Divide the number of students in the class by the number of individuals who will be joining the session in order to create groups. This number will be the number of students in each group. For example, if you have 20 students in your class and five individuals coming to visit, you will need to create five groups of 4 students each. Each group of students will be assigned to an individual.
- Once groups of students have been "assigned" to individuals, ask the groups of students to prepare a list of interview questions they would like to ask. Groups should compose a list of at least eight interview questions. It should be noted that interview questions may also take the form of prompts. Some examples are:
  o Tell me about the time when . . .
  o Explain what it was like when . . .
  o Expand on your experiences with . . .

- Explain to the students that once the interviewees arrive, each group will conduct a group interview with that individual. As such, each student will have the chance to ask at least two questions.
- Once the student groups have drafted their questions, ask them to present the questions to the whole class. Ask the whole group to evaluate the questions. This list of evaluative questions will be helpful during the evaluation:
  o Are the questions open-ended?
  o Will the questions allow the group to gather the information they desire?

o Are there assumptions imbedded into the questions? (e.g., *Where do you like to go out to eat?*—This question includes the assumption that the individual goes out to eat. That may not be the case. Interview questions should be unassuming.)

o Are there "leading" questions? (e.g., *Our teacher is really good; what do you think of him or her?*—This question leads the interviewee toward agreeing with the assessment of the interviewer. Interview questions should not lead the interviewee to respond in a certain way.)

- After the questions have been revised and finalized, ask each group to assign roles to each group member. One person in the group should serve as the greeter/introducer of the interview process. Each and every member of the group should be assigned to ask two or more questions during the interview, and one person in the group should serve as the closer/thanker, to "wrap up" the interview.

- Each group should become familiar with their digital voice recorder. Recording the interviews ensures accuracy. It also serves as an oral record of the interview. Students can be creative in what they use as a digital voice recorder. Digital voice recorders can be purchased, but cell phones, laptops, and other electronic devices also often have recording capabilities. Audio recording devices should be thoroughly tested prior to use. Students may also opt to use two devices to record in the event of a technical failure.

- Encourage students to devise a plan for note-taking during the interview process. Note-taking can help the students gather additional information during the exchange that the audio recorder would not pick up.

- Ask the students to decide on where the interviews will take place. Will each group move to a specific area in the room, or is another location preferable? Consider noise levels and the quality of voice recording.

- Carry out the interviews.

Part 2

- After the interviews have been conducted, have each group listen to their audio recordings. What do they think? Are they satisfied with how the interview progressed? What information shared is the most important? What were the most interesting aspects of the interview? Would different questions have worked better?

- Explain the process of transcription. Transcription is the process of typing up the exact contents (words exchanged) of an interview through the use of word processing software. Explain the utility of transcription to students: It is a way to analyze the interview and to see the conversation in a text-based format. Refer students to captioning for television shows or subtitles on films as a point of reference.

- Assign the transcription of a section of the interview to each student, or allow the groups to assign sections themselves. This should be completed over time and whenever a student has free moments. This could be framed as an anchoring activity. Allow students to experiment with the most efficient ways to transcribe. This might include the use of dictation software (e.g., Dragon Dictation) or audio software (e.g., Audacity).

- Once the transcription is complete, ask the groups to engage in a process of analysis where group members read the transcript, make note of the most salient information shared during the interview, and then negotiate with one another on what information within the interview should be put forward to a wider audience.

- Ask each group to create a product that conveys what was gained through their interview. Employ the RAFT (role, audience, format, topic) strategy, wherein students pick one item from each of the RAFT columns provided on the Interviewing worksheet and use these selections to guide their product creation. Provide students with the Interviewing worksheet.

- Each group will present their product to the whole class.

Differentiation

- Encourage students to conduct life history interviews with an older member of their family. This would involve the construction of interview questions, conducting the interview, audio recording the interview, transcribing the interview, and interpreting the interview.

- Students might also consider completing or attempting to complete a family tree. Online resources such as Ancestry.com (http://www.ancestry.com), FamilyTree.com (http://www.familytree.com), and MyHeritage (http://www.myheritage.com) could be helpful.

- Interview transcripts can be valuable family archives. Students could consider providing copies of the interview (audio and transcripts) to the family member as a gift.

Name: _____   Date: _____

INTERVIEWING

RAFT: Role, Audience, Format, Topic

Directions: Pick **one** from each of the four columns below as you make steps toward the completion of your product. (Note that everyone has the same topic, therefore there is only one option presented in the Topic column.) Use these choices to guide the creation of your product.

Role	Audience	Format	Topic
Nightly news anchor	Students' families	Infographic	
Local government official	Local YMCA patrons	Concept map	
Archivist	High school students	Brochure	
Museum curator	Public library patrons	Poster	
Community educator	Local government officials	Short video	Interview
Newspaper reporter	Local business owners	Advertisement	
Blogger	Local historical society listserv subscribers	T-shirt design	

LESSON 3

Writing Life Histories

Preparation

Purpose: To understand how to write up life histories.

Students Will Understand:
- the process of writing life histories.

Students Will Be Able To:
- write up a life history.

Instructional Strategies Used:
- Guided inquiry
- Group work

Materials Needed:
- Copies of Concept Map Template: Information Collecting handout

Implementation

Time Needed: Varies

Instructions:
- At this time, each student group should have a product based on the RAFT worksheet. The next step is to create a text-based product—a written life history.
- This process involves blending together data collected on a specific individual's life story, such as interview and archival data.
- Ask each student group to review its product from the previous lesson and devise a plan for gathering additional information on the individual's life.
- Within the groups, each student should be assigned to explore a particular source of additional information. Some examples include newspaper articles, websites, photographs (e.g., photo albums or scrapbooks),

archives (e.g., local history archives such as letters, deeds, and other documents), and social media (e.g., public Twitter accounts). The students should use the salient information presented in their products from the previous lesson to drive their pursuit of new information. For example, if the person the students interviewed was a military veteran, it may be helpful for those students to garner information about military service, both locally and in a broad sense.

- Ask each group to create a graphic organizer to express their plan for gathering additional information. The Concept Map Template may be used, or the students can create their own organizer.

- Once the groups have collected additional information about their individuals in addition to the interview data, ask the groups to brainstorm a plan for writing up the life history. The creation of an outline would be helpful. Encourage the students to discuss what the most critical aspects of the story to include might be. The life history cannot include everything. The students, as the authors, must make decisions about what will be contained within the written product and how it will be presented.

- Next, the students must decide how they will co-write an essay that portrays the life history of the person they interviewed in class. The essay writing may take a few days or weeks to complete. You can assign the essay for homework or allow students class time for composition.

- If the students write the essay together remotely or asynchronously, expose them to different ways this might be accomplished, such as by using Google Docs (http://docs.google.com) and Google+ Hangouts (http://www.google.com/+/learnmore/hangouts).

Differentiation

- Encourage students to explore the process of writing up life history by working backward from an existing biography written by a living author. This process involves three steps:
  1. Ask students to locate and read a biography that interests them. This can be done individually or in groups.
  2. Have the students then brainstorm how they think the author collected the information put forward in the biography.
  3. Encourage the students to convert their brainstorm into a polished e-mail message to the author of the biography. The e-mail should include students' questions about how the author carried out the research process.

- If the students are so inclined, encourage them to actually send the e-mail to the author, the author's agent, or the author's publisher. You may want to review the message before it is sent. Then, wait for a response!

- An interesting contemporary example of a life history project is entitled *The Immortal Life of Henrietta Lacks* (information about the book can be found at http://rebeccaskloot.com/the-immortal-life). Not only does this text illustrate life history research, it illustrates issues surrounding the subject's life such as ethical research practices, race, gender, and social class, among many others.

Name:_____ Date: _____

CONCEPT MAP TEMPLATE: INFORMATION COLLECTING

Directions: Students should fill in their names under the information sources that they are planning to explore.

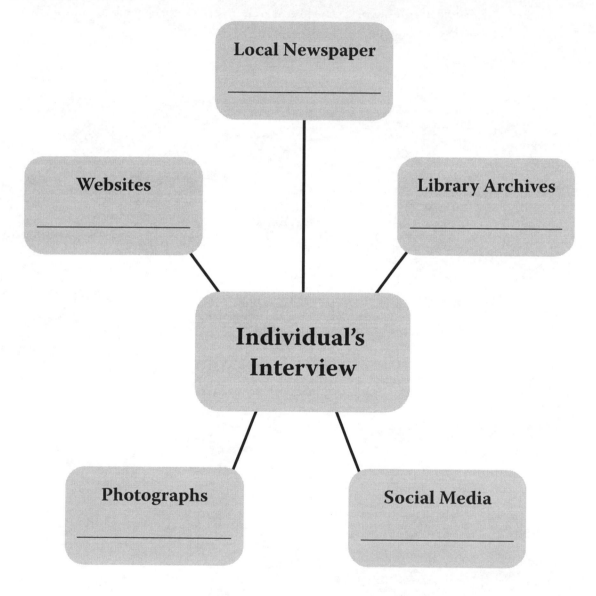

ACTION LESSON 1

Tell Us Your Story

Preparation

Purpose: To conduct life history research with six members of the local community.

Students Will Understand:
- the process of conducting life history research.

Students Will Be Able To:
- conduct life history research.

Instructional Strategies Used:
- Group work

Materials Needed:
- List of suggested interview questions
- Notepad
- Digital voice recorders
- Copies of Life History Research Project handout

Implementation

Time Needed: Varies

Instructions:
- Refer back to the voting completed by the students in the class on the prominent individuals in the community. The top six vote getters will be asked to participate in the life history research project to be completed by the class.
- Students should be broken up into six groups. Each group will be assigned to an individual within the community and will conduct life history research with that person. Talk with the students about the way

they would like to ask their individual to participate in the class research project.

- Work with the students to approach and ask each individual to participate in the project. If any rejections are received, continue down the list of individuals arranged by votes. Ideally, each group will have an individual to work with on the research project. If fewer than six individuals agree to participate, you can rearrange the class into fewer groups to match the number of individuals who have agreed to participate.

- At this time, remind the students of the processes from previous lessons within this unit. Specifically, remind them about the importance of writing effective interview questions, the interview process, ways in which additional data might be gathered to complement life history interviews, and how to make decisions about what to include in life history research essays or papers.

- Allow the students time to create a plan of action for their life history projects. Remind them of the processes their research may include, such as interviewing, transcribing, writing, archival research, photographic research, and field trips. Encourage the students to divide up tasks among group members.

- Provide students with the Life History Research Project: Planning/Progress Report worksheet. You can reuse this worksheet throughout the process to assess the progress of each group.

- Allow time for the students to work on their projects over the course of a few weeks. Periodically ask groups to present their progress to the rest of the class.

- The goal of this part of the process is for students to create a written essay on their individuals. Guide the groups toward this point.

- The overarching goal of this unit is for students to create a website highlighting the people of their community. This site will showcase the students' six (or fewer) life history research projects. Although the students will ultimately be composing essays, ask them to keep records, copies, or files of nontext data they collect, such as photographs, ancillary websites, and other relevant documents.

Differentiation

- Because this life history research project is meant to explore the lives of prominent individuals within a specific community, there may be (unknown) connections between the individuals profiled within the six (or fewer) projects. Encourage students to explore these possible connections by conducting research on these connections. The following questions may be helpful when guiding this line of inquiry:

  o   How might individuals be connected? (e.g., family, workplace, clubs/organizations, neighborhoods)

  o   How would you go about finding these connections?

  o   Through whom might these individuals be connected? (e.g., family, friends, coworkers, teachers)

  o   What is the importance or relevance of the possible relationships between the individuals?

  o   How can individuals' family trees be used to locate connections?

- Ask students to create visual representations of the connections between individuals. This can take any number of forms.

- Recall the overarching goal of the unit: to create a website to house the life histories of prominent individuals within the community. If connections are found between individuals, how might these connections be conveyed through the website? Ask the students to brainstorm creative ways to convert their findings to the site.

- Finally, how might the students engage those who visit the website? For example, how can a more complete web of connections be created among individuals who are a part of this community through an interactive site? In what ways might the site serve as an organic, fluid, and growing repository of both life and local history? Ask the students to plan for creating a website that allows visitors to view it and contribute to it.

LIFE HISTORY RESEARCH PROJECT

Planning/Progress Report

Group Name/Number: _____

Life History (Individual's Name): _____

Name	Task(s)	Date Started	Target Completion Date	Completion Date

ACTION LESSON 2

Taking It to the Web

Preparation

Purpose: To create a website that houses the students' life history projects.

Students Will Understand:
- how to create a website that houses the students' life history projects.

Students Will Be Able To*:*
- create a website that houses their life history projects.

Instructional Strategies Used:
- Think-pair-share
- Group work
- Whole-group discussion
- Workshopping

Materials Needed:
- Computers with Internet access
- Large pieces of paper
- Colored pencils
- Markers
- Magazines
- Scissors
- Glue sticks
- Rulers

Implementation

Time Needed: Varies

Instructions:
Part 1

- The first step in the web design process is for students to understand the tenets of web design. With the ease of free web creation sites (e.g., http://www.weebly.com, http://www.wix.com) no coding skills or HTML language literacy are needed. However, students need to know how to make a site attractive and engaging. They also need to know how to drive visitors to their site and encourage interaction.

- Engage the students in a think-pair-share activity. Allow the students about 15–20 minutes to search the web for information on web design. Each student should compose a list of as many web design tenets as possible. You might suggest they search for these tenets or compose their lists based on websites they frequent. What about these sites make them so attractive, user friendly, and engaging?

- Once the students have composed their lists, ask them to pair up and share their lists with one another. Have the students merge their lists into one large list.

- Then, engage the whole class in the process of making a master list of web design tenets. Compose this master list on the blackboard, whiteboard, or SMART Board; students will use this list as they prepare to create their sites.

Part 2

- Break the students up into small groups. Ask the groups to workshop their ideas for the life history website. Provide them with a variety of resources such as large pieces of paper, colored pencils, markers, magazines, scissors, glue sticks, and rulers. Also provide students with access to the Internet. Ask students to create their mock websites using the large pieces of paper. Each piece of paper represents a page within the site. Ask the students to think about sequencing, navigation buttons, images (be sure permissions are secured), text, and page layout.

- Once the groups have finished their workshop sessions, ask each group to give a brief and informative presentation of their ideas. Ask the students to think about which elements of the groups' websites they like the best. Because the groups have each sketched their pages on individual sheets of paper, you can facilitate the ideas for the final site by combining individual pages from different groups.

- Ask the students about ways to drive users to the site. Would social media be appropriate? If yes, what kinds and how should it be used? Some social media outlets to consider are Facebook, Twitter, and Pinterest.
- Develop a plan to create the final site and any ancillary social media sites. Ask the students to decide on which web-building site they would like to use. You can break the class into groups and assign tasks.
- Ask the class if they would like to host a "reveal party" wherein the final site will go live. They might want to invite the people whose stories are featured on the site.
- Be sure to devise a plan for long-term oversight of the website. Does the site feature a page for comments or blogging? If so, how will that be maintained? If the site includes an e-mail contact, who will monitor the e-mail account? Who will oversee the social media sites, and how? What are the project's next steps, and who will be involved? The site might travel with the students to the next grade, or it might be used with subsequent classes.
- The action components of the lesson (i.e., change, awareness, education) brought about by this lesson will be unique to each implementation. Work with the students in determining the ultimate goal(s) of their work. Who ought to view the site? Why? What action(s) do the students hope to inspire by their work?

Differentiation

Part 1

- Because a large part of action research is action or change through education, it is important for students to think about how to use their new website educationally.
- Ask students to brainstorm ways to use their site to educate their younger peers on their life history research. They should create a short lesson plan wherein their class merges with a kindergarten or first-grade class for the purpose of educating the younger class on their research through the use of the website.
- Help the students think through how they might format their lesson plan. Who will do what? How will they keep all students engaged in the lesson (both classes)? Will they invite a guest speaker? What supplies are needed?
- Ask the students to create a very detailed lesson plan that includes time blocks. They may want to visit a kindergarten or first grade class to get a sense of the class culture within those environments.

- Encourage the students to engage with their younger schoolmates and actually carry out the lesson they created.

Part 2

- After the students have carried out their lesson, ask them to consider whether or not their website was appropriate or user-friendly enough to successfully use with younger children.
- Would another version of the site be more appropriate to use in a situation like the one they just encountered?
- If so, ask the students to browse the web for educational websites created for young children. What are the elements of those sites that differentiate them from the site that they created for their life history research project?
- Ask the students to create a new version of the original site for local teachers to use with their young students.
- The students should create a "package" for these teachers including the lesson plan they created and the new version of the class website. Students can e-mail this package to teachers or deliver it in person.

Unit 4
Photovoice

This unit is designed to teach students the process of doing photovoice research.

What You Will Find in This Unit

PRETEACHING LESSON

How to Take Pictures

Preparation

Purpose: To teach students how to take pictures.

Students Will Understand:
- the basic tenets of what makes a good photograph.

Students Will Be Able To:
- take a picture that is aesthetically pleasing.

Instructional Strategies Used:
- Experiential learning
- Trial and error
- Whole-group discussion
- Guided inquiry
- Cubing

Materials Needed:
- Cameras (one per student)
- Copies of Photography Prompts! handout
- Cubes (construction paper, scissors)
- Copies of Cubing Template handout
- Lamps and string lights (for the cubing activity)
- Magazines and newspapers

Implementation

Time Needed: Varies

Instructions:

Part 1

- Start the lesson by preparing a short slideshow (using PowerPoint) to display various types of photographs. Use a variety of different types of photographs within the presentation: black and white, portraits, landscapes, images from news media, and photographs from various time periods.

- Prepare the students for what they will see by asking them to make note of two things while they view or interact with the photographs:
  1. What elements of the photograph make it appealing?
  2. How do you react to the photographs when you view them?

- Show the students the slideshow and engage them in whole-group discussion. Pose the following questions or prompts to the group:
  - What are the general elements of a "good" photograph?
  - Why do we take pictures?
  - How are photographs used?
  - What does the phrase "A picture is worth a thousand words" mean?
  - What does this quotation mean?
     "We don't see things as they are, we see things as we are." —Anaïs Nin

- Ask the students to search a variety of sources (e.g., websites, magazines, newspapers) and select a few of their favorite photographs. Ask for volunteers among the whole class to show their selections. Ask the volunteers to articulate what elements of the photographs played into their selections. In other words, what makes the photographs their favorites?

- Next, break the whole class into small groups. Ask them to engage in a show-and-tell session regarding the photographs. How did they make their selections? Are there commonalities among group members? Lastly, ask the groups to create a list of attributes they feel best describe a "good" or aesthetically pleasing photograph.

- Once the groups have composed their lists, engage the whole class in the creation of a larger list that encompasses all of the groups' work. After the larger list is established, question the class about topics and terms such as *subjectivity, relativism,* and *taste*. Pose questions such as *If a photograph is blurry, does that mean it is of poor quality? Why or why not?* Explain why some photographers would *want* to create blurry photographs. Explain that beauty and aesthetics are culturally bound. Something considered beautiful in one context, culture, or country might not be considered beautiful in another.

Part 2

- Brainstorm a way to provide your students with cameras of some kind. For the purposes of this lesson, digital cameras are best. Camera phones will work. The cameras can be very simple.
- Provide the students with the Photography Prompts! handout. Ask them to pick a few of the prompts and take some photographs in response to each of the prompts they select.
- Depending on the resources to which you have access, you will either have the students create a digital or physical display of their photographs. In addition, have the students self-evaluate their photographs based upon the large list of attributes they felt best described a "good" or aesthetically pleasing photograph, which they created in Part 1.
- If your students create digital displays—they could use PowerPoint, Prezi (http://www.prezi.com), Jux (http://www.jux.com), or any other digital presentation format—have them present their photographs to one another in small groups. If your students create physical displays, have them create the displays so that other members of the class can easily engage with the photographs. For example, students may want to post their photographs to trifold poster boards or create their own photo albums or scrapbooks.
- Once the students have the chance to view each other's photographs, ask for volunteers to describe something they learned from their classmates' photographs related to aesthetics. For example, perhaps a student took a photograph of his or her toothbrush from a unique angle or in an interesting context. Maybe another student in the class did not take a photograph of his or her toothbrush because it seemed like a simple object and therefore not worthy of photography. In addition, you may want to ask the students to articulate how their classmates' photographs impacted them or made them feel.

Differentiation

- In the event that some students have extra time during the implementation of this lesson, have them engage in a cubing anchoring activity. Later in this unit, students will organize a photography exhibition, so elements of this cubing activity will support that end goal.

- Use the Cubing Template to create an anchoring activity for your students. This activity will require students to experiment with different ways of presenting photographs. It will also challenge students to think about why photographers would opt to manipulate their images or present them in a specific manner. There are many ways to manipulate and display photographs. We live in a visual culture and many people (students included) narrate their lives visually through social media. Examples such as Facebook, Twitter, Instagram, Pinterest, Flickr, and Tumblr are illustrative. The digital images posted to these sites are often manipulated through smartphone apps and other software.

- Cut out the cube and use tape to put it together. Have students roll the cube and carry out the directive on the side that is facing the ceiling.

PHOTOGRAPHY PROMPTS!

Take a picture of your toothbrush.

Take a picture of something you walk past regularly.

Take a picture of one of your meals.

Take a picture of one of your friends.

Take a picture of something in nature.

Take a picture of something that's your favorite color.

Take a picture of a car, van, or truck.

Take a picture of your favorite school supply.

Take a picture of a building.

Take a picture of some clouds.

Take a picture outside at night.

Take a picture of something made of glass.

Take a picture of water.

Take the most creative picture you can think of to take.

CUBING TEMPLATE

Use a variety of construction paper pieces to create a mat for your printed photograph.

Create a Pinterest board of online articles about and images of photography exhibitions in museums.

Using one digital image, create 10 Powerpoint slides that display the image in different ways.

Hang one of your printed images on the wall of your classroom. Illuminate the photograph in different ways. What do you like best?

Compose an e-mail to a local photographer to invite him or her to come to the class and discuss his or her work.

Google "online photo editor" and experiment with a few. Which do you like best and why?

LESSON 1

What Is Photovoice?

Preparation

Purpose: To teach students about photovoice.

Students Will Know:

- **Photovoice** (noun): A participatory action research method. Photovoice researchers ask participants to respond to questions or prompts through photographs. Then, participants narrate the contents of those photographs in focus groups or interviews facilitated by the researcher or member of the research team. One result of photovoice research is a photovoice exhibition. The goal of the exhibition is to reach policy makers regarding the topics brought forward through the research (Wang & Burris, 1997).

Students Will Understand:

- the basic tenets of photovoice.

Students Will Be Able To:

- articulate the definition and purpose of photovoice.

Instructional Strategies Used:

- YouTube video
- Web exploration
- Direct instruction
- Whole-group discussion
- Guided inquiry
- Stations

Materials Needed:

- A book or books on participatory photography, such as *Portraits and Dreams* by Wendy Ewald or *Lives Turned Upside Down: Homeless Children in Their Own Words and Photographs* by Jim Hubbard
- "Photovoice: From Snapshots to Civic Action" video (http://www.youtube.com/watch?v=l4zAdktMUNg)
- Local newspaper (a few hard copies)

- Copies of Station Signs A-F
- Computers with Internet access

Implementation

Time Needed: Varies

Instructions*:*

Part 1

- Prepare for this lesson by setting up six stations or centers in different areas of your classroom. Make copies of the signs (or handouts) that explain each station to the groups. Post the signs around the room; an example of how the room might be set up can be found below. Aim to have the students physically move from station to station. The six stations will be as follows:

  A) Participatory documentary photography book reviewing. What do you think?

  B) Discussion prompt: Describe photovoice in your own words.

  C) What is more important in photovoice—the photos or the voices? Why?

  D) In what ways can photographs impact people in ways that words cannot?

  E) Take a look at today's local newspaper. What's the most attention-getting thing you see and why?

  F) Imagine the circus is coming to town! Describe how photographs taken by the circus performers and those of your local newspaper's reporters might be different.

A) Place the station sign here, along with the books by Wendy Ewald and Jim Hubbard.	B) Place the station sign here.	C) Place the station sign here.
D) Place the station sign here.	E) Place the station sign here, along with a few hard copies of the local newspaper.	F) Place the station sign here.

Part 2

- Begin the lesson by showing the students a video called "Photovoice: From Snapshots to Civic Action" (see the Materials Needed section for the link).
- Then, ask the students to explore the PhotoVoice website (http://photovoice.org). This can be done individually, in pairs, in small groups, or as a whole class.
- Ask the students to share their initial reactions to this new method of action research: photovoice.
- Provide the students with a short minilecture on photovoice using the information provided in the Students Will Know section.
- Ask the students to think about research topics and/or questions that might be best addressed through photovoice. Discuss these ideas as a whole group.

Part 3

- Separate the class into six groups. Explain the station activity. Each group will start at a particular station, carry out the activity at the station, and then rotate to the next one. There are six stations in total. Groups will have a set amount of time for each rotation (around 3 minutes).
- Use a stopwatch (or you can display an online timer) to keep time, and be sure the students are aware of the time. If you allocate 3 minutes per station, the activity will take approximately 18 minutes.
- Once each group has visited each station, engage the whole group in a discussion about each station.

Differentiation

- The photovoice methodology assumes a sighted participant. There may be, however, potential photovoice participants who are blind or visually impaired. How can photovoice projects be constructed so as to be as accessible as possible for folks with disabilities of all kinds? Ask students to think about this.
- Have students create a list of guidelines for making photovoice project participation accessible to all individuals. This list, or product, can take any form (e.g., flyer, booklet, brochure, short video). The audience for this product is photovoice researchers.
- Ask the students to explore the Sensory Photography section of the PhotoVoice website (http://www.photovoice.org/html/pvmethodology/method_04/index.htm). Ask your students, *What is sensory photography?*

- Also ask students to brainstorm other forms of disability along with how they might best accommodate folks with various disabilities so those individuals are able to participate.
- If time allows, encourage the students to do a web search on the Americans with Disabilities Act (see http://www.dol.gov/dol/topic/disability/ada.htm). How might this assist them in their list of guidelines?

Show & Tell!

Take a look at the book or books at this station, and then discuss the following questions as a group:

» **What do you think of these books?**

» **How are they like or unlike a photovoice project?**

» **Which images do you like best? Why?**

Group Discussion!

Describe photovoice in your own words.

Group Discussion!

What is more important in photovoice—the photos or the voices?

Why?

Group Discussion!

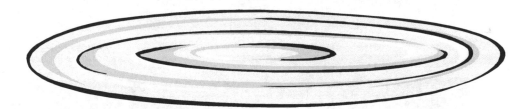

How can photographs impact people in ways that words cannot?

Provide some examples.

Show & Tell!

Take a look at today's local newspaper.

What's the most attention-getting thing you see and why?

Imagination Station!

Imagine the circus is coming to town!

Describe how photographs taken by the circus performers and those of your local newspaper's reporters might be different.

LESSON 2

Picture Stories

Preparation

Purpose: To teach students about the process of narrating photographs.

Students Will Understand:
- how to create narrations for photographs they have taken.

Students Will Be Able To:
- articulate the purpose of photograph narration as it relates to the photovoice method.

Instructional Strategies Used:
- Scrapbooking and/or digital storytelling

Materials Needed:
- Scrapbooking materials (e.g., scissors, glue, various paper, stickers, markers, pens, pencils, tape)
- Cameras
- Camera Usage Planning Document

Implementation

Time Needed: Varies (this lesson may take place over the course of several days or weeks)

Instructions:
Part 1
- Start the lesson by asking students to brainstorm an upcoming event in which they are participating or attending. This event might be related to school, but it does not have to be. Some examples might be a field trip, neighborhood picnic, orchestra concert, sporting event, museum trip, meal at a relative's or friend's home, nature walk, visit to the local park, or any other event, large or small.

- Ask the students to narrow their lists of events by thinking about an event they would like to document through a scrapbook or digital story. Again, this does not have to be a major event, just something the student would like to remember and document.

- Tell the students they ought to select an event at which they feel comfortable taking photographs. They will be documenting the event through photographs and the creation of captions or narrations of those photographs. There is one critical rule, however: They are *not* allowed to take photographs of people. They may take photographs of landscapes, objects, and anything other than people. Creativity is essential in the documentary photography process, and so will be the second step—narrating those images.

- Once the students have decided on an event to document, have them devise a plan for photography. The ultimate goal is to create a scrapbook or digital story that conveys the "essence" of the event. There is one other parameter to which the students must abide in creating their work: they can include only 12 photographs in their scrapbooks or digital stories. They may, however, take as many photographs as they like during the process of photography during the event. Encourage the students to be creative and make use of metaphor, symbolism, abstraction, staging, perspective, and intentionality.

- Devise a plan so that all students have access to some type of camera during the event they have selected. You can use the Camera Usage Planning Document to help.

- Because the students' events will occur at different times, you should think about how to plan due dates and in-class work time.

Part 2

- Once the students have attended their event and taken photographs, encourage them to think about and plan for how to convert their images into a scrapbook or digital story that documents the event. Depending on the event, students may want to give their product to someone as a gift. Encourage them to think about the audience and the message(s) they hope to send through their work.

- A simple Internet search can generate a lot of great scrapbooking ideas. Scrapbook.com (http://www.scrapbook.com) is a good place to start.

- Students can use a variety of tools to create a digital story. The Center for Digital Storytelling (http://www.storycenter.org) is a great resource for students interested in creating a digital story. PowerPoint, Prezi, VoiceThread (http://www.voicethread.com), Microsoft Photo Story, iMovie, and Blogger (http://www.blogger.com) are all viable software options for students to use.

- Remind the students they can only use 12 of their photographs, so they should be selective in their planning. Also, the captions or narrations they use for the images should not be overly verbose—just long enough to convey the meaning of the photographs.
- Once the students have completed their scrapbooks or digital stories, provide time for them to interact with one another's work.
- Finally, ask students to reflect on the process of creating their scrapbooks or digital videos. This can be facilitated with the whole group. Here are some reflective questions to ask of the students:
  o What was it like to take photos at your event?
  o Was it difficult to take photos that did not include people? Why or why not?
  o What was it like to create narrations or captions for your photographs?
  o How did you decide how to organize your scrapbook or digital story?
  o What were you trying to portray with your scrapbook or digital story?
  o What about your classmates' scrapbooks or digital stories did you enjoy most?
  o What will you do with your scrapbook or digital story?

Differentiation

- If you have a group of students who complete this assignment very early or who seem to have really enjoyed the digital storytelling element of the last lesson, engage them in a group digital storytelling endeavor.
- Ask the students to identify a school event they would like to document for that group or for the school in a general sense. Some examples might be a sporting event or season, a guest speaker, a fundraising event, a parade, a graduation, a theatrical performance, a choral performance, or a school dance.
- Encourage the group to decide upon roles for each of the group members. Also encourage the students to seek out input from those directly involved with the event to see what their needs are in terms of documenting the event. The digital story may be used to promote next year's event, serve as an advertising tool, or be duplicated and sold to raise money for the group.
- Advise the group members to use what they learned in the previous lesson to create their new digital story. Students will have to make decisions about photographs, images, effects, captions, music, colors, and timing.

- Encourage the students to involve members of the event's sponsoring group to view the digital story and offer feedback before the final version of the product is created.

CAMERA USAGE PLANNING DOCUMENT

Student Name	Event to Document	Date of Event	Camera Plan

LESSON 3

Who Are You?

Preparation

Purpose: To teach students about the process of participating in a photovoice project.

Students Will Understand:
- the complexities related to participating in a photovoice project.

Students Will Be Able To:
- articulate the process of participating in a photovoice project.

Instructional Strategies Used:
- Guided discussion
- Autophotography
- Focus groups
- Digital storytelling

Materials Needed:
- Cameras
- Copies of PechaKucha Event Evaluation Planning Tool handout

Implementation

Time Needed: Varies (this lesson may take place over the course of several days or weeks)

Instructions:
- Start the lesson by telling the students they will be engaging in a small-scale, self-focused photovoice project. Students will be engaging in a process termed autophotography (Combs & Ziller, 1977), which is similar to other related forms of self-expression such as autobiography.
- Each student will take a designated number of photos in response to both of the following questions:

    o Who are you?

    o Who are you not?

    You can limit the number of photos students take in response to each prompt based on any number of factors including class size, access to cameras, or length of time allotted to this lesson. If using digital cameras, it would be difficult to limit the number of photos taken, but ask students to select a limited number of images to use for the project among their larger pool of images.

- Tell the students they are not allowed to take photos of people in their responses to the prompts. This is in accordance with image ethics (Gross, Katz, & Ruby, 1988) and makes for a safer photography experience for students.

- Derive a plan to ensure that all students have access to some type of camera prior to engaging in this lesson. The quality of the camera and images are less important than the students' experiences with the process of engaging in a small-scale and self-focused photovoice project.

- Encourage the students to think deeply and creatively about their approaches to this project. Suggest the use of metaphor, abstraction, staging, perspective, and manipulation (e.g., decoloring an image) through the photography process. Remove students' perceptions of any sort of boundaries with this project. You may, however, want to put forward some guidelines, such as no photographs of anything illegal or pornographic. Consider the student group with whom you are working as you think through the best way to approach this aspect of the lesson.

- Allow the students about a week to take the photos. During that time frame, ask the students to report on the process. How are they going about the photography? What have they photographed? On what is the process causing them to reflect? Are they thinking about themselves in any new ways? What has been fun about the project? What has been challenging about the project?

- Once the students have completed the process of photography, ask them to share their images with classmates in pairs or small groups. As the students engage in the sharing process, ask them to document some of the most salient words, phrases, or whole sentences they are using to articulate and explain the meanings of the images. They can do this through note-taking or using some form of digital voice recording. Dictation software would also be an appropriate option for this process.

- Once the students have their images selected and narrations of those images in written form, the students should then begin the process of crafting their digital auto-stories. For this particular lesson, all students will create their stories using a similar format. Refer to the PechaKucha

20x20 website (http://www.pechakucha.org). The PechaKucha format involves showing 20 images for 20 seconds each, giving students time to talk about each image; students will use this as a guide when choosing their format. Inform the students that they will be having their own version of a PechaKucha event during the school day.

- As a whole group, have the students discuss and jointly decide upon a format for the digital auto-stories. An easy place to start may be to consider the following:
  o What format/software will be used? (e.g., PowerPoint)
  o How many images will be used in each story? (e.g., six from each prompt)
  o How will words be incorporated into each story? (e.g., each image will be followed by a narration or each image will also include a narration)
  o How many seconds will be designated to each slide? (e.g., 20 seconds per slide)
  o Will voice narration be used? Will music overlay the presentations?

- Once the students have established their parameters for the digital auto-stories, provide them with time to complete the work. This can also be assigned as homework if the students have access to needed technologies outside of school.
- Work with the students to establish the best day and time to host the PechaKucha event. How will their work be shared? Who will be invited? How will they model the event based on what they learned from the PechaKucha website? What logistical decisions need to be made related to the event?
- Ask the students what they might gain from the event. How might they evaluate the success of the event? What are the risks associated with the event?
- Carry out the event and enlist the help of students throughout the entire process.
- After the conclusion of the event, engage the class in an evaluative process. This can be done through small and large group discussions. How might an event similar to this one be improved in the future? What worked well? What did not work?
- The final lesson with this unit involves a photovoice exhibition. Ask a student or a group of students to document the evaluative process as well as the lessons learned.

Differentiation

- If some students complete their digital auto-stories early or are in need of additional challenge, encourage a student group to devise and carry out an evaluation plan for the PechaKucha event using the PechaKucha Event Evaluation Planning Tool worksheet.

- Explain to the students that they will soon be hosting a photovoice exhibition. This PechaKucha event, while very valuable and important, can be viewed as a pilot for the larger, more complex and comprehensive photovoice exhibition.

- Encourage students to use what they learned about survey research to create one or two surveys to use as evaluative tools related to the PechaKucha event. For example, they may want to survey the class members to gain their insights, and they may also want to generate a separate survey for PechaKucha event guests. Both perspectives are valuable.

- Ask students to think of other ways they might gather data or feedback on the perceived successes of the event. How might the event be documented so that successful elements are replicated during the photovoice exhibition?

- Encourage the students to use the PechaKucha Event Evaluation Planning Tool in their efforts. Once the evaluation is complete, ask this student group to report out their findings to the whole class.

Name:_____   Date:_____

PECHAKUCHA EVENT EVALUATION PLANNING TOOL

Directions: Complete the prompts inside each box. Then compose a fluid evaluation plan based on this planning document.

What/who are your sources of data within this evaluation plan? On what is success measured?	Describe the methods you will use to collect evaluative data.

Describe which methods will be used with which data sources (e.g., photographs will be taken during the event: photo documentation is the method and the happenings of the event are the data source). Also, how is success measured differentially based on the various combinations of data sources and methods?

How will you analyze your data?	In what ways could you explain or present your analysis of the data (e.g., charts, graphs, prose)?

How will you present the analysis and findings to your classmates?

ACTION LESSON 1

Strengths and Weaknesses

Preparation

Purpose: To teach students how to carry out a photovoice project.

Students Will Understand:
- the steps, details, and logistics involved in carrying out a photovoice project.

Students Will Be Able To:
- carry out a photovoice project

Instructional Strategies Used:
- Whole-group instruction
- Guided discussion
- Experiential learning
- Focus groups
- Committee work/work in small research teams

Materials Needed:
- Cameras
- Copies of Photovoice Project Committee Planning Document handout

Implementation

Time Needed: Varies (this lesson may take place over the course of several days or weeks)

Instructions:
- Start the lesson by telling the students that they will be working together to carry out a photovoice project. Throughout the course of this photovoice project, the students will take on dual roles as both researchers and participants. The purpose of this photovoice project is to bring awareness to the perceived strengths and weaknesses of the school's

surrounding community. Depending on your location, you can make determinations about what geopolitical area your class will focus on during this project. For example, if your school is situated in a city or town where all of the students live, you might focus your project on that specific city or town. However, if your students are from a wide variety of cities and/or towns, you may want to narrow your focus to the immediate area around the school. You can certainly enlist the help of your students in this decision-making process. All of the steps in this lesson should be modified based on input from the students.

- Once the community of focus is determined, review the following with your students:
  o the basic tenets of the photovoice method;
  o the previous lessons within this unit. Ask students to recount what they have learned and how that learning can assist them in carrying out a photovoice project; and
  o the most recent lesson. Ask students to think about how a photovoice project will work with other participants in addition to themselves.

- Explain to the students the focus of the project: understanding student perceptions of the community of focus. Remind the students that the purpose of this photovoice project, specifically, is to bring awareness to the perceived strengths and weaknesses of the school's surrounding community.

- Work with the students to determine the following:
  o How many participants should be involved in the project? (And from which grades?) Keep this number relatively small.
  o How will participants be recruited (e.g., "shoulder taps," teacher recommendations, flyers)?
  o What prompts will be used? (Two simple prompts could be *What are the strengths of this community?* and *What are the weaknesses of this community?*)
  o How many photographs will each participant take?
  o How will participants take the photos (e.g., disposable cameras, digital cameras, camera phones)?
  o How will narrations of those photographs be generated (by each photographer/participant) and documented (e.g., audio recording, writings)? Students may opt for interviews, focus groups, or another form of participant engagement, which could also be digital, such as a blog or other online platform.
  o How will participants be trained with regard to photography? *No photographs of individuals are permissible*—this is an important parameter.

- Once those determinations have been made, break up the class into small groups, or committees, each tasked with different aspects of the project. For example, you may want to create the following committees: recruitment, training, interviews/focus groups, equipment, and mentors (these committee members can assist the participants who are not in the class).

- Provide each committee with time to meet and discuss their ideas and action steps as well as a tentative timeline. Use the Photovoice Project Committee Planning Document as needed.

- Guide each committee through their action steps and provide time for each committee to report out to all other members of the class on a regular basis (a few times per week if necessary—the more communication among and between the committees, the better).

- Remind all committees that all members of the class are participants in the project as well as researchers.

- One way the class and larger participant group may want to engage in photography is to host a "photowalk" through the community of focus. During this walk, all participants can opt to take photos for the project. Although this may be a helpful idea, it is important to give participants time for their photography so unique photographs can be generated. Students will have lots of ideas about what to photograph based specifically on where they live and where they go within the community.

- The next step in the photovoice process is a photovoice exhibition, which will be outlined in the next action lesson.

Differentiation

- Based on the size of the community of focus, you may want to designate a committee of students to engage in a map-making activity based upon where photographs were taken within the community.

- Students may opt to create their map from scratch or explore and use map-making software online. Google Map Maker (http://www.google.com/mapmaker) may be a viable starting point.

- Ask the students to think about the next iteration of this project: a photovoice exhibition. The purpose of the exhibition is to bring about awareness of the students' perceptions of their community. Ideally, this exhibition will gain the attention of policy makers, who have the power and influence to make positive change with the community. Encourage the students to consider this and how the inclusion of a map-based display might help the class reach its goal of gaining the attention of policy makers.

- The students should create their map display for the purposes of gaining the attention of policy makers during the exhibition. With this in mind, challenge them to create the most intriguing and meaningful display that they can.

Name: _____   Date: _____

PHOTOVOICE PROJECT COMMITTEE PLANNING DOCUMENT

Committee	Action Item	Completion Date	Action Item	Completion Date	Action Item	Completion Date
Recruitment						
Training						
Interview/ Focus Groups						
Equipment						
Mentors						

ACTION LESSON 2

Photographer's Exhibition

Preparation

Purpose: To teach students how to host a photovoice exhibition.

Students Will Understand:
- the steps, details, and logistics involved in hosting a photovoice exhibition.

Students Will Be Able To:
- host a photovoice exhibition.

Instructional Strategies Used:
- Whole-group instruction
- Guided discussion
- Field trip or guest speaker
- Experiential learning
- Committee work/work in small research teams

Materials Needed:
- Photography display materials (e.g., matting, poster board, posters, screen, and LCD projector)
- Copies of exhibition programs
- Other materials related to the exhibition (depending on how you choose to organize it)
- Copies of Photovoice Exhibition Committee Planning Document handout

Implementation

Time Needed: Varies (this lesson may take place over the course of several days or weeks)

Instructions:
Part 1

- The next step/lesson within this unit is the photovoice exhibition. This component of the project is meant to showcase the students' work, bring awareness to the students' perceptions of the strengths and weaknesses of their community, and reach policy makers within the community who may be able to enact change based on the contents of the exhibition.

- When the data collection phase of the photovoice project is completed, the students will begin preparing for the exhibition with your guidance. Additionally, this should be a participatory event, so student participants outside of the class should have some level of involvement in the exhibition planning, to the extent at which they are comfortable. Keep this in mind as you go forward with the lesson.

- Students may not have had previous experience with photography exhibitions. It may be important for students to be exposed to such an exhibition. Discuss the possibilities of a field trip with students.

- Are there any local museums, libraries, or other places that regularly host photography exhibitions? Is there a local photography studio or camera shop willing to host the students for a field trip? Would a local (or regional) photographer be willing to come to the classroom to talk with the students about how to organize exhibitions? Would a conversation between the (regional) photographer and the students via Skype be possible? Would a museum curator be another viable option as a guest speaker?

- Work together with the students to arrange some type of field trip or guest speaker experience. Ask the students to prepare for this experience by thinking about questions they would like to ask and things they need to learn in order to create and host an effective exhibition.

- Once the field trip or guest speaker event has taken place, ask the students to collectively document their learning. This could be orchestrated in any number of ways, such as a Twitter backchannel, wiki, shared word processing document, or writing a list on the board and then taking a photograph of the list.

Part 2

- The next step of this lesson is the planning, execution, and evaluation of the photovoice exhibition. If the committee work from the last lesson worked well, you can implement that tactic within this lesson also.
- Below is a list of questions that must be addressed during the planning process. These questions can be collapsed into categories and addressed through student committee work if the previous experience was positive. If not, guided, whole-group discussions with the class will work also.
  o Who will make what decisions related to the exhibition?
  o How will the exhibition be funded? How much will it cost?
  o Where will the exhibition take place?
    » What are the policies related to the place? (e.g., food, wall hangings, attendees)

  o When will the exhibition take place?
    » Will there be an opening?
    » Will the exhibition remain? If so, for how long—a day, a week, a month, a year?

  o Who will be invited to the exhibition?
  o How will the event be publicized?
    » Will social media be used? If so, how?
    » Is outside help needed for publicity (e.g., from parents, local businesses)?

  o What will happen during the exhibition?
  o Will food and drink be served during the event? If so, how will that be arranged?
  o How will the space be arranged and decorated?
  o How will the photographs and text be presented? In what format (e.g., actual photographs, digital displays)?
  o Who will do what during the exhibition?
  o If the project participants are at the exhibition, will attendees know who they are? How?
  o Will you ask for attendee feedback in any way? If so, how?
  o How will you evaluate the success of the event (e.g., attendee surveys, comment cards, specific number of attendees), and what must be done during the event to facilitate that process?
  o How will documents (e.g., flyers, guest sign-in sheets, an exhibition program) related to the exhibition be stored and shared? Consider utilizing shared-access online storage space such as Dropbox (https://www.dropbox.com) or Google Drive (https://drive.google.com).

- Once the method for addressing these questions has been decided, action steps must be taken. Again, this can be done through committee work or others means, based on your past experiences with the class. The Photovoice Exhibition Committee Planning Document is included to help students prepare; use this document as needed, and complete and revise the document for your purposes.
- Specifics of this lesson and the photovoice exhibition will vary greatly depending on a number of factors. As such, additional details are not provided within this lesson.

Differentiation

- Although you may designate a committee of students to create and carry out an evaluation of the photovoice exhibition, it may also be helpful to plan for an assessment of long-term impacts of the event/exhibition.
- Designate individual students or a group of students to brainstorm ways to assess the impact of the photovoice exhibition over time. For example, on the guest sign-in sheet at the event, you might ask for guests' e-mail addresses. Guests could be e-mailed with a link to an online survey (see previous unit on survey research) to assess the ways in which the exhibition has and/or is impacting them. If local policy makers attended the event (e.g., city mayor, school board members, school principal, local business leaders), students could compose and send personal letters to those individuals to request an interview about their perceptions of the event. Ask students to be creative regarding how they approach this endeavor.
- Students should also brainstorm ways in which the contents of the exhibition might be reorganized and re-presented in another way or through another means. Is another exhibition possible at another location? If the first exhibition was hosted at the school, maybe the next one could be held at the local public library, community college, or recreation center? Would a student-created video (such as the YouTube video referenced at the start of this unit) be a viable way to present the photovoice project to a larger audience? If so, what are the steps needed to create such a video? What about a website?
- Finally, how might any positive impacts of the exhibition (in terms of positive change) be showcased? For example, if students took photos of cigarette butts outside the school grounds and explained that these images represent high numbers of teens smoking—which the students argued was a weakness in the community—how was the issue subsequently addressed? Were policy makers influenced to do something

based on the students' presentation? Did positive change result? How can this be measured or assessed? How can these positive changes be shared with the larger community?

Name:_____ Date: _____

PHOTOVOICE EXHIBITION COMMITTEE PLANNING DOCUMENT

Committee	Action Item	Completion Date	Action Item	Completion Date	Action Item	Completion Date

Unit 5
Playbulding

This unit is designed to teach students the process of playbuilding as qualitative research.

What You Will Find in This Unit

PRETEACHING LESSON

What Is a Play?

Preparation

Purpose: To teach students about the intricacies, components, and types of plays.

Students Will Know:
- **Tragedy** (noun): A play based on some form of human suffering and/or a series of tragic events; it typically has an unhappy ending.
- **Comedy** (noun): A play intended to make the audience laugh; it typically has a happy ending.
- **Farce** (noun): A play intended to be humorous; it includes ridiculously improbable situations and exaggerated characters.
- **Satire** (noun): A play intended to be humorous; it includes the use of wit, irony, and sarcasm and is meant to expose human vice or folly.
- **Musical** (noun): A play in which music, song, and dance are dominant.
- **Historical Account** (noun): A play rooted in actual historical events.

Students Will Understand:
- the intricacies of and comprehensive components necessary for a successful play or theatrical performance, and
- the differentiating features that distinguish different types of plays.

Students Will Be Able To:
- explain the steps necessary for a successful play or theatrical performance, the roles of those involved with a successful theatrical performance, and what differentiates different types of plays from one another.

Instructional Strategies Used:
- Whole-group instruction
- Guided discussion
- Field trip

Materials Needed:
- Copies of What Is a Play?: Preassessment
- What Is a Play?: Preassessment Rubric

- Copies of Observation Template handout
- Copies of What Is a Play? Choice Board handout

Implementation

Time Needed: Varies (this lesson may take place over the course of several days or weeks)

Instructions:
Part 1
- Explain to the students that you are interested in learning about what they already know about plays. Provide each student with the preassessment. Allow the students about 10 minutes to complete it. Use the rubric to score the preassessment. This exercise will give you a general sense about what your students already know. It will help you know where to begin your instruction.
- Depending upon your students' prior knowledge about plays, decide whether or not a basic overview of the concept is needed. If needed, explain that plays are typically written by playwrights, and their work is meant to be acted out in a public fashion. Plays are typically directed and actors are cast to play various parts within the performance. Staging for plays can be very elaborate or rather simplistic, depending on both the play and the budget. Plays take place on Broadway (http://www.broadway.com) and Off-Broadway (http://www.offbroadway.com/home) in New York City, as well as at regional theaters, at community theaters, and in schools and houses of worship all across the country. Plays involve music to varying degrees, and they can take the form of tragedies, comedies, farces, satires, musicals, or historical accounts.

Part 2
- Contact your local community or university theater. Establish a day and time when you can arrange a field trip for your class to attend a play. In addition, inquire about the possibility of the class being able to meet those involved in the production, including directors, actors, set designers, musical directors, musicians, lighting technicians, ushers, ticket sales personnel, and graphic designers.
- Explain to the students that the field trip to the play will be an active, rather than a passive, experience. Put differently, students will not attend to simply watch the play. They will be actively seeking out an understanding of what components go into the total production.

- Prepare students to be active observers during the field trip by providing them with the Observation Template. This worksheet can be used during the field trip to help students analyze the things they notice.
- If the field trip involves only attending a play, provide the students with copies of the Observation Template to complete throughout the experience. If the field trip involves attending the play and engaging in conversation with people involved in the production, also prepare students to ask questions during the exchanges. Ask students to brainstorm ahead of time. They should be prepared to ask thoughtful questions to advance their thinking about how a play comes to fruition.
- Once the students are back in a classroom setting (after the field trip), prepare them to discuss what they learned through the experience.

Part 3

- Break up the class into small groups and ask them to share the contents of their Observation Templates.
- As a whole group, discuss the contents of each group's observations related to each of the eight boxes within the template. Be very specific throughout the conversation. In addition, ask the students if they enjoyed the experience and why (or why not).
- Ask the students to reflect upon their conversations with those involved in the production, if applicable. What stood out to them most? What was most surprising? Again, encourage the students to be very specific.
- Ask the students to imagine hosting a play, either at the school or elsewhere. What about the play they watched would they like to emulate? Why?
- Encourage the students to create a master list of play "best practices" related to their field trip experience.
- Let the students know they are preparing to host their very own production within forthcoming lessons connected to this unit.

Differentiation

- Encourage students who have particular interest in this topic to complete a "winning" combination of exercises on the What Is a Play? Choice Board.
- Either collect students' work, ask them to present their work to the class or in small groups, or ask them to complete the work as an anchoring activity.
- Students' work can be used simply as an activity or for a grade.

Name:_____ Date: _____

WHAT IS A PLAY?

Preassessment

1. In the space below, provide a response to the following question: *What is a play?* Incorporate the following five words in your response: *playwright, characters, performance, script,* and *director.*

2. Where do plays typically take place? List as many places as you can.

3. What are some different types of plays? List as many types as you can.

WHAT IS A PLAY?

Preassessment Rubric

	5	4	3	2	1	0	Points Earned
Item 1	All five words were used properly within the context of a logical paragraph.	Four words were used properly within the context of a logical paragraph.	Three words were used properly within the context of a logical paragraph.	Two words were used properly within the context of a logical paragraph.	One word was used properly within the context of a logical paragraph.	No words were used within the context of a logical paragraph.	
Item 2	N/A	N/A	Three or more places were listed.	Two places were listed.	One place was listed.	No places were listed.	
Item 3	N/A	N/A	Three or more types were listed.	Two types were listed.	One type was listed.	No types were listed.	
Comments:						**Total Points Earned:**	_____ /(11)

Name: _____ Date: _____

OBSERVATION TEMPLATE

What did you notice about the ticketing process and the playbill?	**What did you notice about the venue?**
What did you notice about the music, acoustics, and/or sound effects?	**What did you notice about the set?**
What did you notice about the actors and their costumes?	**What did you notice about the audience?**
What did you notice about the play itself?	**What else about this experience did you notice?**

Name:_____ Date:_____

WHAT IS A PLAY? CHOICE BOARD

Create a timeline that outlines the history of the Tony Awards. Within your timeline, be sure to include a variety of graphics and photographs. Use the Tony Awards website (http://www.tonyawards.com) as a starting point.	Create a table that outlines all of Shakespeare's plays and categorizes them based on type. In addition, create a brief one-paragraph summary of each play.	Research current Broadway plays or shows. Create a dynamic playbill for one of the Broadway shows you researched and found particularly interesting.
Imagine the play you watched during the field trip was going to be held inside your classroom. Draw plans for the conversion of your classroom into a theater and make a list of items you would need in order to successfully convert the room into a suitable space to host the play.	Think about a book or short story you have recently read for school. How might that book or short story be converted into a play? Create a short, three-act play that converts the book or short story into a play that can be acted out.	Conduct a web scavenger hunt on the word *amphitheater* (or *amphitheatre*). What is an amphitheater and what is its history? Convert your findings into a PowerPoint or Prezi presentation.
Research stage lighting techniques and draft a stage lighting plan for an actor's monologue within a play. You can do this in one of two ways: sketch out the stage lighting plans on a piece of sketch paper, or arrange an area of your classroom for this performance by making use of available lighting in the classroom such as lamps or string lights.	Think about a recent funny exchange you had with a classmate, friend, or family member. Convert that exchange into a very short play. Write out the play and include staging, character sketches, and any other ancillary information.	Conduct a web search of the term *improvisational theater*. Create a variety of scenes, characters, and topics to be acted out by members of the class.

LESSON 1

Acting 101

Preparation

Purpose: To teach students about the basic tenets of acting.

Students Will Know:
- **Projecting** (verb): To direct one's voice so it can be heard at a distance.
- **Enunciating** (verb): To say or pronounce clearly.

Students Will Understand:
- the basic tenets of acting.

Students Will Be Able To:
- explain the basic tenets of acting, and
- play a role (however small) in a small-scale, in-house play.

Instructional Strategies Used:
- Whole-group instruction
- Whole-group discussion
- Experiential learning
- Guest speaker
- Workshopping
- Scene creation and acting

Materials Needed:
- Copies of Acting 101: Preassessment handout
- Acting 101: Preassessment Scoring Key
- Copies of Stage Directions Key handout
- Copies of Prompts for Scene Creation handout

Implementation

Time Needed:
- *Part 1:* Approximately 45 minutes

- *Part 2*: Approximately 1 hour
- *Part 3*: Varies

Instructions:
Part 1

- Explain to the students that you are interested in what they know about acting. Distribute the preassessment, and ask the students to complete it. The preassessment should take the students about 10 minutes to complete.
- Allow the results of the preassessment to guide your entry point for the lesson. If necessary, generate a whole-group instructional session to convey the terms and ideas put forward within the preassessment.
- Provide students with a copy of the Stage Directions Key.
- Ask students to brainstorm other important components of stage acting in addition to the ones listed on the preassessment (breathing, projecting, enunciating, listening, watching, and memorizing).
- Pose the following questions to the class to generate a whole-group discussion:
  - In what ways do you already "act" in your life?
  - How important are the following when acting: being natural, having fun, and embodying your character?
  - How would you go about researching your character for a certain play?
  - Imagine there is a mishap during the performance of a play (e.g., lines are misspoken, an actor drops a prop, there is a long silence). If you were on stage, what would you do?

Part 2

- Identify a local stage actor. This could be an actor affiliated with a community theater program or a local college or a university student majoring in theater or active with the theater program.
- Contact this individual to inquire about a visit to your class for a workshop. Explain that you are interested in having your students interact with a local actor to prepare to create their own production.
- Ask the actor to prepare a short minilecture on the basics of acting. Then, allow time for the students to ask questions. Finally, ask the actor to take the students through some basic acting exercises.

Part 3

- Break up the class into groups of three.
- Provide each group with a scene creation prompt. You can use the prompts provided on the Prompts for Scene Creation handout or

generate your own. The prompts should be random so as to generate creativity among the groups.

- Ask each group to sketch out a scene related to the prompt. Each member of the group should have a role with lines in the scene.

- Designate an area within the classroom as the stage. Ask each group to perform its scene on stage. Ask each group to provide the audience (i.e., other students) with their prompt before they begin.

- You might consider providing each group with a time limit for its performance. One to 3 minutes would be appropriate.

- After the miniperformances, engage the whole group in a discussion about what they noticed. What worked? In what ways did the students embody the tenets of acting?

- Remind the students, again, that you are preparing them to create and host their own production, which will be a form of playbuilding—a participatory action research methodology.

Differentiation

- For students particularly interested in acting, encourage them to work together to build an improvisational acting game for the whole class to play.

- Ask students to search the Internet for improvisational acting exercises. An example is the "simple task" improvisational exercise, which can be performed as follows:
  o Inform the actors they will be acting out a simple task such as sending a text message, walking down the hallway, or reading a book.
  o Allow each actor to choose a simple task to act out. Give the actors a few moments to think about their performances.
  o Ask the actors to give their performances, one at a time. Provide a time limit.
  o Then, ask the audience to provide each actor with the next simple task he or she will perform. For example, if the actor was sending a text message in his or her performance, the next act could be to receive a text message.
  o Ask the actors to give their second round of performances based on the audience members' input.
  o Finally, ask the audience to provide each actor with a third and final simple task to perform. To continue the example above, the next simple task could be to turn off the cell phone in exasperation.

o Once the entire series of simple tasks has been acted out, break up the class into small groups to talk through the following discussion questions:

» What were you thinking as you prepared for each performance?

» Why did you use certain emotions, facial expressions, gestures, and postures in the performance?

» What about the experience felt comfortable or easy?

» What about the experience felt uncomfortable or difficult?

▪ Have the students work together to design a game that incorporates these improvisational acting exercises. The game should be designed so the entire class can play, either as a whole group or in small groups. The purpose of the game should be for students to practice their acting skills and to build their capacity for creativity through "spur of the moment" acting.

ACTING 101

Preassessment

Match the following terms related to acting with their definitions.

_____ 1. Stage Left   A. Toward the ceiling

_____ 2. Stage Right   B. Actor's left

_____ 3. Upstage   C. Toward the back of the stage (away from the audience)

_____ 4. Downstage   D. Toward the floor

_____ 5. Above   E. Actor's right

_____ 6. Below   F. Across the stage—upstage or downstage

_____ 7. Diagonal   G. Toward the front of the stage (toward the audience)

Explain why the following are critically important to stage acting.

1. Breathing

2. Projecting

3. Enunciating

4. Listening

5. Watching

6. Memorizing

ACTING 101

Preassessment Scoring Key

Match the following terms related to acting with their definition. (**7 points possible**)

__B__ 1. Stage Left	A. Toward the ceiling	
__E__ 2. Stage Right	B. Actor's left	
__C__ 3. Upstage	C. Toward the back of the stage (away from the audience)	
__G__ 4. Downstage	D. Toward the floor	
__A__ 5. Above	E. Actor's right	
__D__ 6. Below	F. Across the stage—upstage or downstage	
__F__ 7. Diagonal	G. Toward the front of the stage (toward the audience)	

Explain why the following are critically important to stage acting. (**6 points possible**)
Example correct responses are provided below.

1. Breathing
   Take deep breaths before speaking while acting on state. Being out of breath or breathing erratically can seem unnatural to the audience.

2. Projecting
   Speak loudly and clearly. Audience members sitting in the back of the venue must be able to hear you. Pretend you are outside.

3. Enunciating
   Pronounce the words within your lines clearly. The audience must understand what you are saying.

4. Listening
   Listen to the other actors as well as any music or sound effects. This will help you be totally aware of what is happening on stage.

5. Watching
   Watch the other actors on stage. This will help you adjust your own movements as necessary.

6. Memorizing
   Know your lines. Memorizing your lines is critical for stage acting.

STAGE DIRECTIONS KEY

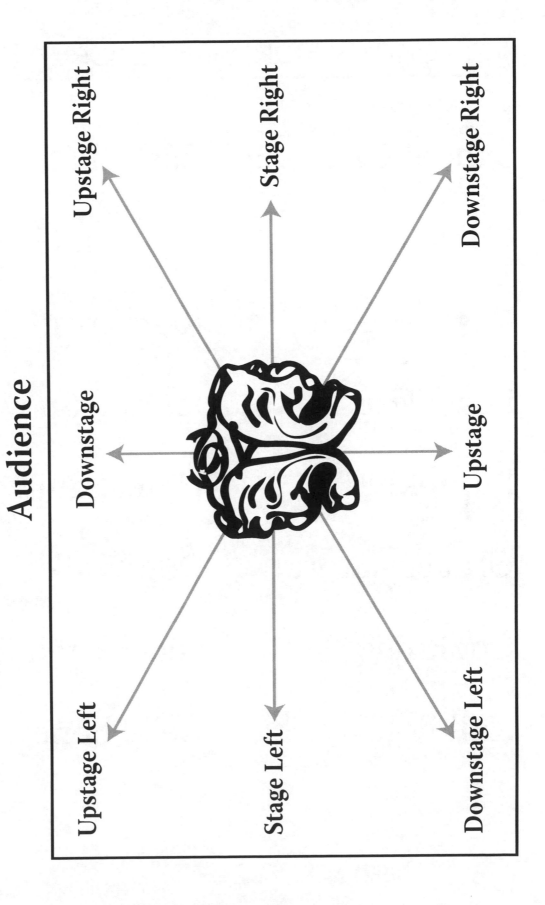

Audience

Downstage

Upstage Right

Stage Right

Downstage Right

Upstage Left

Stage Left

Downstage Left

Upstage

PROMPTS FOR SCENE CREATION

School Cafeteria	Basketball Shoes
Carnival	Football Game
Bowling Alley	Rainforest
Road Trip	Ice and Snow
Pumpkin Patch	Hand Sanitizer
Grocery Store	Dog Walk
Cooking	Pencils and Pens
Nail Polish	Cell Phone

LESSON 2

Stage Design 101

Preparation

Purpose: To teach students about the basic tenets of stage design.

Students Will Understand:
- the basic tenets of stage design.

Students Will Be Able To:
- explain the basic tenets of stage design, and
- work as a part of a team (however small) in a small-scale in-house play to brainstorm, build, and maintain the stage design.

Instructional Strategies Used:
- Web-based scavenger hunt
- Social bookmarking
- Wiki creation
- Experiential learning
- RAFT (role, audience, format, topic)

Materials Needed:
- Copies of Web-Based Scavenger Hunt handout
- Copies of Stage Design 101: RAFT handout
- Shoeboxes
- Construction paper
- Scissors
- Glue
- Various types of small objects students can use in the creation of a diorama (e.g., cotton balls, pipe cleaners, buttons)
- Various materials for students to use in the creation of their products while doing the RAFT activity (e.g., modeling clay, yarn, popsicle sticks, paint)
- Cardboard boxes
- Fabric
- Brown lunch bags
- Old (clean) socks

- Needle and thread
- Computers with Internet access

Implementation

Time Needed:
- *Part 1*: Varies
- *Part 2*: Approximately 1 hour
- *Part 3*: Varies

Instructions:

Part 1

- Tell the students they are going to be learning about the basic tenets of stage design through the process of creating various types of products related to stage design. But first the students will engage in a web-based scavenger hunt to identify helpful websites for use during the stage design process.
- Break the students up into five groups:
  o Stage Design Theory
  o Scenic Design and Drawing
  o Lighting
  o Props
  o Construction

- Ask each group to locate at least 10 helpful websites related to its specific subtopic within the larger topic of stage design. Provide students with the Web-Based Scavenger Hunt worksheet to log their work. Within the Annotations column, the students should provide a sentence or two describing each website they locate.
- The next step in this part of the lesson is to create a Pinterest (http://pinterest.com) account to house all websites located by the five groups. At least 50 websites should have been located throughout the process. Those who are unfamiliar with Pinterest can learn more about it on the website's About page (http://pinterest.com/about), and signing up can be done easily from the home page. If you are not familiar or comfortable with using Pinterest, you can opt to use another social bookmarking platform. Having all of the sites in one location will be helpful for the entire class as they go forward. Other examples of social bookmarking sites include Delicious (http://www.delicious.com) and Diigo (http://www.diigo.com).

Part 2

- Now that a large collection of websites related to stage design has been created, the students must work to distill the vast amount of information into something more usable in terms of size and format. As such, the students will work together to assess the most valuable information housed within each of the websites. They will then move that critical information into a wiki, which will be organized in an easy-to-use format.

- You can opt to encourage students to use one of two platforms: Wikispaces (http://www.wikispaces.com) or Google Sites (http://www.google.com/sites/help/intl/en/overview.html). There are other wiki platforms from which to choose as well.

- Because the students have already been broken up into groups, keep the students within their groups as they work through this process.

- Once the students have completed their work on the wiki, ask each group to give an informal minipresentation of their work within the wiki, focusing on the most important aspects.

- For Part 3 of this lesson, all students must have access to all of the information gathered—both the wiki and the social bookmarking site.

Part 3

- The final part of this lesson involves a RAFT (role, audience, format, topic) activity.

- Students will select one item from each of the four columns and then create a product accordingly. Note: The role and audience choices must be different.

- Once each student has created his or her product, ask each of the students to provide a short presentation of his or her work to the whole class.

Differentiation

- For students particularly interested in the stage design aspect of theatrical performance or for those who complete the RAFT activity early, introduce students to puppetry. Ask the group to locate and view some YouTube clips from *The Muppet Show*. Then, ask the students to consider how stage design for puppet shows and puppetry differs from traditional stage acting.

- Either individually or in groups, have the students build a puppet show stage with a specific self-selected theme. Students can build their stages for their own use or inquire with one of the kindergarten or lower elementary grade teachers to see if a stage could be built and used within that teacher's classroom in the school for the students to use.

- Encourage students to use the Internet to research how puppet stages are designed and built.
- If there is a lot of interest in this particular form of acting, encourage the students to take the next step in the process and create puppets for the purpose of performing some type of puppet show. Provide students with ample materials from which to work. Encourage students to bring items from home as well.

LESSON 2

Stage Design 101

Preparation

Purpose: To teach students about the basic tenets of stage design.

Students Will Understand:
- the basic tenets of stage design.

Students Will Be Able To:
- explain the basic tenets of stage design, and
- work as a part of a team (however small) in a small-scale in-house play to brainstorm, build, and maintain the stage design.

Instructional Strategies Used:
- Web-based scavenger hunt
- Social bookmarking
- Wiki creation
- Experiential learning
- RAFT (role, audience, format, topic)

Materials Needed:
- Copies of Web-Based Scavenger Hunt handout
- Copies of Stage Design 101: RAFT handout
- Shoeboxes
- Construction paper
- Scissors
- Glue
- Various types of small objects students can use in the creation of a diorama (e.g., cotton balls, pipe cleaners, buttons)
- Various materials for students to use in the creation of their products while doing the RAFT activity (e.g., modeling clay, yarn, popsicle sticks, paint)
- Cardboard boxes
- Fabric
- Brown lunch bags
- Old (clean) socks

- Needle and thread
- Computers with Internet access

Implementation

Time Needed:
- *Part 1*: Varies
- *Part 2*: Approximately 1 hour
- *Part 3*: Varies

Instructions:

Part 1

- Tell the students they are going to be learning about the basic tenets of stage design through the process of creating various types of products related to stage design. But first the students will engage in a web-based scavenger hunt to identify helpful websites for use during the stage design process.
- Break the students up into five groups:
  o Stage Design Theory
  o Scenic Design and Drawing
  o Lighting
  o Props
  o Construction

- Ask each group to locate at least 10 helpful websites related to its specific subtopic within the larger topic of stage design. Provide students with the Web-Based Scavenger Hunt worksheet to log their work. Within the Annotations column, the students should provide a sentence or two describing each website they locate.
- The next step in this part of the lesson is to create a Pinterest (http://pinterest.com) account to house all websites located by the five groups. At least 50 websites should have been located throughout the process. Those who are unfamiliar with Pinterest can learn more about it on the website's About page (http://pinterest.com/about), and signing up can be done easily from the home page. If you are not familiar or comfortable with using Pinterest, you can opt to use another social bookmarking platform. Having all of the sites in one location will be helpful for the entire class as they go forward. Other examples of social bookmarking sites include Delicious (http://www.delicious.com) and Diigo (http://www.diigo.com).

WEB-BASED SCAVENGER HUNT

Website Title	URL	Annotations

STAGE DESIGN 101

RAFT: Role, Audience, Format, Topic

Directions: Pick **one** from each of the four columns below as you make steps toward the completion of your product. Note: The role and audience choices must be different.

Role	Audience	Format	Topic
Mural artist	Mural artist	PowerPoint presentation	Stage lighting plan for a series of monologues
Electrician	Electrician	Brochure	Stage design for a play set in a kitchen
Stage design theorist	Stage design theorist	Diorama	Props for a play involving a beach
Theatre director	Theatre director		Scenic design for a play set in an enchanted forest
Architect	Architect		Stage lighting plan for a play set at night
Carpenter	Carpenter		Background mural for a play set in an urban environment
Graphic designer	Graphic designer	Model(s)	Props for a play set inside a zoo
Musical director	Musical director	Poster/blueprint	Accessibility plan for an actor who uses a wheelchair

LESSON 3

To Be a Playwright

Preparation

Purpose: To teach students how to compose a small-scale play.

Students Will Know:
- **The Aristotelian Elements of a Play** (noun): Six essential elements of drama, as identified by Aristotle in his *Poetics*. The elements consist of the following:
  - *Plot*—Arrangement of the events that take place on stage
  - *Character*—Architects of the plot; provide the vehicles for the events that take place on stage
  - *Theme*—Impetus for playwright's work; element of life the play-wright explores within the plot and through the characters
  - *Language*—Dialogue between characters within the play; creates a means for expression
  - *Rhythm*—Timing, pacing, and sequencing of the plot, created through the characters' use of language and action around a theme
  - *Spectacle*—All things seen and heard on stage

Students Will Understand:
- the basic tenets of how to write a play.

Students Will Be Able To:
- write a small-scale play.

Instructional Strategies Used:
- Whole-group discussion
- Experiential learning

Materials Needed:
- Copies of a short play
- Copies of Aristotelian Elements of a Play handout
- Copies of A Play Script Dissected handout
- A 12-sided die and a six-sided die
- Copies of Characters and Themes—Roll 'em! handout

Implementation

Time Needed:
- *Part 1*: Approximately 35 minutes
- *Part 2*: Approximately 55 minutes
- *Part 3*: Varies

Instructions:

Part 1
- Provide the students with a copy of a short play. You might consider combining this lesson with a language arts lesson focused on the study of plays.
- Ask the students to take a few moments to read the play silently, and then engage them in a whole-group discussion about the specific ways the play is like and unlike the readings in which they typically engage. For example, ask the students to think about this play in particular and compare and contrast it with books, magazines, newspapers, websites, and so on. How is it similar? How is it different?
- Ask two students in the class to write these lists on the board (one for similarities and one for differences), or you can compose a two-column table within a word processing document and project it onto a screen.
- Ask the students follow-up questions related to this exercise. For example, ask the students why a playwright would use a different format than a novelist. Ask the students how they would go about converting a short novel into a play. Throughout that process, what would be lost and what might be gained? Ask the students about their experiences with reading a book and then watching the movie version of that book. You might use *Charlotte's Web* as an example. When a book is adapted to film, what is lost and what is gained? How is this conversion process similar to and different from adapting a book into a play for theatrical performance? Who should make decisions about how this is done?
- Next, introduce students to the Aristotelian Elements of a Play handout. A description of the six elements can be found in the Students Will Know section.
- Ask the students to complete the worksheet based on the play you handed out and in accordance to the elements above.
- Once the students have completed the worksheet, engage in a whole-group discussion about the students' work. Which elements were confusing? Which elements seemed simple? What types of processes do you think playwrights go through in the preparation of their work? How might those processes incorporate these six elements?

Part 2

- After completing Part 1, tell the students they are now going to engage in a brief playwriting workshop.

- The students will be randomly assigned two elements from a prebuilt list: characters and theme. Students will have to generate the remaining four elements of the play on their own: plot, language, rhythm, and spectacle.

- Before starting the workshop, provide students with the A Play Script Dissected handout. This handout is an "annotated" play script that illustrates one way (among many) that students can choose to arrange their play (i.e., with dialogue and stage directions). Ask students to brainstorm potential ways to format their play script.

- Then, each student will roll a 12-sided die to determine his or her characters twice and a six-sided die to determine his or her theme once for a short play script he or she will compose. If no actual dice are available, virtual dice can be found at http://www.bgfl.org/bgfl/custom/resources_ftp/client_ftp/ks1/maths/dice.

- Provide the students with some brainstorming time to consider their plot, language, rhythm, and spectacle.

- Students may opt to sketch out their plays as outlines or concept maps before actually typing or writing them. Allow time for this also.

- Once each student has composed his or her play script (which should not be very long—one or two pages maximum) ask for volunteers to have their play scripts shown on the screen. Take the student volunteers through the process of explaining his or her work and include a discussion of the six Aristotelian Elements as well as formatting choice. Go through several of the students' plays in this way.

Part 3

- Now that the students have had experience in being playwrights, provide them with the opportunity to compose a play of their very own design. Give students the option to convert an existing story into a play or to compose an entirely new piece.

- Ask them to consider what they have learned and incorporate their learning into this new piece.

- This part of the lesson can also be coupled with another unrelated lesson. For example, consider combining this play-writing exercise with a history report, short biography, or even a laboratory report.

- Encourage maximum creativity with this assignment!

Differentiation

- Differentiating this lesson can take several forms. You could:
    o Suggest students develop a cover page, act and scene index, and character sketch pages for their plays.
    o Encourage deeper levels of character development though complex dialogue.
    o Suggest students bring their plays to "life" with a selected animation website or software such as Muvizu (http://www.muvizu.com), GoAnimate (http://goanimate.com), Dvolver Moviemaker (http://www.dvolver.com/moviemaker/make.html), or Xtranormal (http://www.xtranormal.com).
    o Suggest students identify partners and act out one another's two-character plays.
    o Have students roll the 12-sided die again and write another character into their plays.

- If some students complete their plays early, you could place them into a group and challenge them to find a way to connect the individual plays (or scenes) into one play (with several scenes and/or acts). This would potentially require some additional writing.

ARISTOTELIAN ELEMENTS
OF A PLAY

Plot: What happens in this play?	**Character:** Give a brief description of the characters in this play.
Theme: What is this play about?	**Language:** How is language used in this play?
Rhythm: Describe the rhythms within this play.	**Spectacle:** What would you expect to see and hear during this play?

CHARACTERS AND THEMES—ROLL 'EM!

 Use a 12-sided die. Roll your die twice. Your characters will be determined by the roll of the die! See the key below. If you roll the same number twice, you will develop your play script with two of the same characters. But you will have to find a way to make each of them unique!

Characters:

1: Police officer

2: Store clerk

3: Chess master

4. Pastry chef

5: Politician

6: Professional writer

7: Retired person who volunteers within the community regularly

8: Young man with a broken arm

9: Athlete

10: Librarian

11: Gardener

12: Business professional

Now use a six-sided die. Roll your die once. Your theme will be determined by the roll of the die! See the key below.

Themes:

1: Forgiveness for a wrong

2: Joys of learning something new

3: Helping another person

4: Benefits of taking risks

5: Transitional moment in life

6: Taking time for family and friends

ACTION LESSON 1

What It Means to Be Us

Preparation

Purpose: To teach students how to begin the playbuilding process.

Students Will Know:

- **Playbuilding** (noun): An action researcher methodology. Throughout the playbuilding process (Norris, 2009), data are generated and analyzed in a similar fashion to most other qualitative research processes. The dissemination, however, typically occurs as a theatrical performance. And, typically, the data generation, analysis, and (re-) dissemination are all done simultaneously within the theatrical performance.

Students Will Understand:

- the basic tenets of playbuilding as well as how to begin the process.

Students Will Be Able To:

- explain playbuilding as an action research methodology and process, and
- begin the playbuilding process, which includes brainstorming, initial data gathering, analysis, meaning-making, and initial dissemination through play writing, stage design, and theatrical performance.

Instructional Strategies Used:

- Whole-group discussion
- Individual writing
- Group writing
- Experiential learning
- Peer review

Materials Needed:

- 3" x 5" index cards (three per student)

Implementation

Time Needed:
- *Part 1*: Approximately 45 minutes
- *Part 2*: Approximately 60 minutes
- *Part 3*: Varies

Instructions:
Part 1
- At this time, students should have a strong command of basic concepts related to acting, stage design, and play writing. The final two lessons within this unit will shift the students' focus to playbuilding (Norris, 2009) as an action research methodology and process. For a definition of playbuilding, see the Students Will Know section. Note that playbuilding includes data generation and analysis (at some level) within the performance; this sets it apart from other performance-based qualitative research approaches such as ethnodrama (Saldaña, 2005). The Joe Norris Playbuilding website (http://www.joenorrisplaybuilding.ca) is a great resource for more information.

- The goal of this lesson is to engage students in the initial playbuilding processes; the goal of the next lesson is to take the play to the stage and, as such, the playbuilding circle will be closed upon the completion of the final lesson with this unit.

- This lesson can be carried out with your whole class or a smaller student group (e.g., student club or organization). First, introduce playbuilding as a concept. Then, tell the students they are going to develop an action research project using the playbuilding methodology. Explain the overarching topic you have in mind: *What it means to be us.* (This topic can be modified to meet your and your students' specific needs. For example, you may be preparing for Bullying Awareness Week at your school. Playbuilding could be a really powerful way to address bullying.) You will first have to come to a group understanding of "us." How does this group collectively self-identify? The self-identification could be anything, yet there should be some level of specificity. For example, do all members of the group identify as sixth-grade students? Environmental Club members? Drama Club members?

- Once a group-wide understanding of "us" is established, ask the individual students to compose a short vignette or story that addresses the prompt, *What it means to be us.* If the group identifies as sixth-grade students, you might assist the students in their writing with specific prompts or questions, such as the following:
  o What is it like to have to change classrooms for different classes?

     o   What was it like to go from the oldest to the youngest in the school?

     o   What is it like to walk through the hallways with older students?

Part 2

- Once the students have completed the composition of their vignettes, provide each student with a 3" x 5" index card.

- Ask for volunteers to either read aloud or summarize their vignettes for the remainder of the group. If there is enough time for everyone in the group to share, that is ideal. Encourage members of the group to share, but do not make this mandatory.

- As members of the group are sharing their vignettes, ask the others in the group to jot down ideas onto their index cards related to the theme or themes (see previous lesson for an explanation of themes) within each vignette. In other words, ask the students to think about what the story is about and then write that theme on their card. For example, if a student writes about how different sixth grade is as compared to fifth grade, a theme might be termed *transitions in school*, *growing up*, or simply *change*.

- After all volunteers have read or shared their vignettes and notes have been jotted on the cards, ask all group members to share what they have written on their cards and create a master list of themes on the board or screen. This master list should be kept for future use. Explain to the students that this process is both data collection and data analysis.

- Once the master list of themes has been generated, collectively review the list to see if any of the themes can be combined into one theme.

- Now that a number of themes have been generated regarding the prompt *What it means to be us*, engage the group in some discussion around consensus building. Which of the themes on the shortened list most saliently address the prompt? Which of the themes are most emblematic of the students' experiences, challenges, and triumphs?

- If consensus building around the themes becomes cumbersome, you might forecast ahead and tell the students the final step of the play-building process: hosting a play production. Ask the students to imagine hosting a play with some number of acts and scenes. If the title of the play is *What It Means to Be Us*, what might those acts and scenes look like (while keeping the themes generated through the vignette-writing process in mind)? If this process remains cumbersome, you could designate some number of themes (e.g., 3-8) and ask the students to vote.

Part 3

- Once the themes are established, break up the class or group into smaller groups—one group for each theme.
- Each group is responsible for composing a short play based on its theme. The vignettes can serve as material for the construction of each play, but the plays do not have to be modeled on the vignettes exclusively. Students should keep in mind the things they learned in Lesson 3 of this unit throughout the writing process.
- At the end of this lesson, a number of small plays should be generated— one for each of the themes in response to the prompt *What it means to be us.*

Differentiation

- Differentiating this lesson can take several forms. You could:
  o Vary the manner in which the data are collected. Instead of vignette writing, any number of methods could be substituted. Ask the students to brainstorm some other ways they could address the prompt.
  o If some students have musical talent or interest, encourage them to imbed self-composed music, songs (of all kinds—raps, jingles, solos), and/or sound effects into their plays.
  o Encourage very detailed and rich descriptions of scenes, stage design, and character costumes.

- If some groups finish early, encourage them to engage in peer review processes between groups. Ask each reviewing group to assess the other group's play based on the six Aristotelian Elements of a Play and offer feedback in accordance with those six elements. Questions should be asked of each group, such as:
  o How can the language use be modified so as to further emphasize the theme?
  o Is each character fully developed? If no, why not? What would make further development possible?
  o Is the scene appropriate for the plot?
  o Will the theme be obvious to the audience? Why or why not?
  o Is the climax of the play placed in the best location within the plot? Why or why not?
  o Are more or less characters needed? Why or why not?
  o Is the play paced well? Why or why not?

ACTION LESSON 2

Going Live

Preparation

Purpose: To teach students how to complete the playbuilding process.

Students Will Understand:
- the basic tenets of playbuilding as well as how to complete the process through a dramatic performance or series of dramatic performances.

Students Will Be Able To:
- complete the playbuilding process, which includes initial dissemination of the data generated around the prompt through completing the play-writing process, stage design, and theatrical performance. It also includes additional data collection through the initial dramatic performance and in various ways after the dramatic performance. Final plans for disseminating research findings must be made and carried out in order to complete the playbuilding process.

Instructional Strategies Used:
- Whole-group discussion
- Group writing
- Experiential learning
- Dramatic performance

Materials Needed:
- All items necessary for the dramatic performance

Implementation

Time Needed: Varies (this lesson may take place over the course of several days or weeks)

Instructions:
Part 1 (Preproduction)

- The students now have created some number of small plays linked to each one of the themes generated during the data collection process of vignette writing in response to a prompt.

- Allow each group time to present its play to the remainder of the class. View this process as a large workshop. What about each play can or should be revised, rethought, or redone?

- At this time, review the vision for the dramatic performance of the plays, which will next be converted into a comprehensive performance, as a whole. The purpose of the dramatic performance is to display the findings of the inquiry into the prompt, *What it means to be us*. The merits of this action research process are twofold: It allows a student group to express itself in a meaningful way and it allows onlookers (i.e., the audience) to better understand the student group that is giving the performance. It should also be noted that the audience must be engaged in the data collection in some way either before, during, or after the performance (or any combination of the three) to allow the performing group to ascertain additional insights into the prompt.

- Engage the groups in some decision-making exercises regarding how to arrange or organize the series of short plays into one performance or larger play. Remind the students that plays typically are organized as some number of acts, and acts are comprised of scenes. What kind of organization of the current number of short plays makes the most sense? Can any of the existing plays be collapsed into one? What else must be done to ensure smooth transitions from one smaller unit to the next?

- Once these decisions are made, break up the class or group into committees assigned to various aspects of the play production. These committees may include:
  o *Play Writing*—Will add finishing touches to the play including a cover page, scene index, page numbers, and other needed writing
  o *Stage Design and Scenery*—Will secure a space for the performance and create/design the stage area and scenery
  o *Logistics*—Will organize the day and time for the performance; contact any actors from outside the class such as students in other classes or groups, parents or guardians, and teachers or school staff; and contact any necessary volunteers to assist with the production such as a lighting crew, musicians, ushers, and concessions stand personnel
  o *Costumes*—Will gather or make any necessary costumes
  o *Promotions*—Will create advertising materials and a playbill for the event

o *Audience Engagement and Research*—Will consider how to keep the audience engaged during the performance and arrange for audience data collection activities before, during, and after the performance, which could include pre- and postperformance surveys, clicker technology during the performance, or a Twitter backchannel

o *Documentation*—Will video record the performance, take photographs during the performance, and partner with the Audience Engagement and Research committee to securely and accurately collect data gathered during the performance

- Provide an overview of the duties and responsibilities of each group. Also, set aside designated times for the whole class or group to meet to report progress and communicate between committees.

Part 2 (Rehearsal)

- As the performance details come into focus through the committee work, rehearsals for the play must begin.
- Inquire with your group about who would like to do what during the actual performance. It may be that all of the students want to be actors within the performance, but some students may not be interested in performing. Students should not be made to act, but each student should have some role (acting or nonacting) in the event during the actual performance. Examples of nonacting roles might be working with the lighting crew, overseeing the data collection efforts, or taking photographs of the event for documentation purposes.
- There should not be a need to host auditions; there should be enough characters in the play so that everyone can play a character if they want to. Make sure the students know who is playing which character.
- You may opt to take on the role of director or seek out a volunteer for this position. Moreover, you may not want to be the director for every act or scene within the play. Consider inviting others into the preparation phase of the performance. You might reach out to the local civic or university theater for assistance with this endeavor.
- During the rehearsals, give the students ample freedom to modify the play as needed to really emphasize the theme within each scene or act. Give students permission to improvise and experiment with their lines, posture, voice, and so on.
- As components of the stage design and scene are created, add them to the rehearsal space. Spend rehearsal time on stage as much as possible.

Part 3 (Production)

- As the performance date draws close, meet with each committee to be briefed on its progress and offer any help needed.
- Gather the whole class or group to review all details related to the performance. Give time to each committee to report on its progress. Allow the committees to ask and answer questions.
- Give special attention to the group assigned to Audience Engagement and Research. How, specifically, will new data be generated and collected during the performance? Some specific ideas include the following:
  o Include a survey (see Unit 1) with the play invitation to preassess the audience. Be sure to connect your data-gathering initiatives to the overarching topic of the inquiry or play and to the themes generated by the class concerning that topic.
  o Use clicker technology to ask questions of the audience during the performance. Part of the stage design could include a projector screen. You could also use Poll Everywhere (http://www.polleverywhere.com) and allow the audience to respond via text message.
  o Invite audience members onstage during the performance and ask them what they would do if they were certain characters in certain situations.
  o Provide a postperformance survey inside the playbill.
  o Invite audience members to stay after the performance to engage in small-group discussions or focus groups about the topic.

- Once a comprehensive plan is built for the performance, host the event!

Part 4 (Debriefing)

- Shortly after the event is over, it is critical to reconvene the class or group to debrief the experience and make sense of the new data collected. Next steps related to the research process should be plotted also.
- Give each person within the class or group the opportunity to share his or her reflections about the performance. Some probing questions might include the following:
  o What did you enjoy most about the performance?
  o What did you enjoy least about the performance?
  o What about the performance surprised you most?
  o Did things go as you expected? Why or why not?
  o What should we have done differently?
  o What did you learn during the performance?
  o What did you notice about the audience?
  o How are you presently envisioning the impact of the performance on the audience?

- Give ample time to the Audience Engagement and Research committee to present and discuss its work during the evening. What data was collected and what steps are necessary to analyze the collected data (if it is not already analyzed)? What does the new data tell us about the performance?
- Guide the whole class or group in a discussion about what next steps should be taken with regard to dissemination of the new data from the performance. Perhaps you polled the audience about its knowledge of or experiences with bullying during the performance. How should those data be presented? Perhaps you asked the audience what it learned during the performance through a postperformance survey. How should those data be presented?
- The next steps of the data dissemination process may include a whole host of options such as the creation of a PowerPoint presentation to be used in other classes, the creation of a comic book that represents the performance and data collected, the creation of a digital story that puts forward the most important aspects of the project, or the production of another dramatic performance that builds upon the original.

Differentiation

- Differentiating this lesson can take several forms. If you allow students to self-select their committee involvement, differentiation may occur naturally. Despite this, you could:
  o Encourage a variety of dramatic forms within the play, such as puppetry, mime, and simulation (as in a game show where audience members come to the stage).
  o Designate a committee to specifically create a digital story or documentary film that encapsulates the entire playbuilding process.
  o Allow students to self-select side projects related to the performance and playbuilding process overall. For example, if a particular individual within the community provides many volunteer hours to the endeavor, a student may wish to make a photo collage or other memento for that volunteer.

References

Atkinson, R. (1998). *The life story interview*. Thousand Oaks, CA: Sage.

Bogdan, R. C., & Biklen, S. K. (2007). *Qualitative research for education: An introduction to theories and methods* (5th ed.). Boston, MA: Pearson.

Combs, J. M., & Ziller, R. C. (1977). Photographic self-concept of counselees. *Journal of Counseling Psychology, 24,* 452–455.

Glanz, J. (1998). *Action research: An educational leader's guide to school improvement*. Norwood, MA: Christopher-Gordon.

Gross, L., Katz, J. S., & Ruby, J. (Eds.). (1998). *Image ethics: The moral rights of subjects in photographs, film, and television*. New York, NY: Oxford University Press.

Goodson, I., & Sikes, P. (2001). *Life history research in educational settings: Learning from lives*. New York, NY: Open University Press.

Latz, A. O., & Adams, C. M. (2011). Critical differentiation and the twice oppressed: Social class and giftedness. *Journal for the Education of the Gifted, 34,* 773–789.

Norris, J. (2009). *Playbuilding as qualitative research: A participatory arts-based approach*. Walnut Creek, CA: Left Coast.

Sagor, R. (2005). *The action research guidebook: A four-step process for educators and school teams*. Thousand Oaks, CA: Corwin Press.

Saldaña, J. (2005). *Ethnodrama: An anthology of reality theatre*. Toronto, CA: AltaMira Press.

Stringer, E. (2007). *Action research* (3rd ed.). Thousand Oaks, CA: Sage.

Wang, C. C., & Burris, M. A. (1997). Photovoice: Concept, methodology, and use for participatory needs assessment. *Health Education and Behavior, 24,* 369–387.

About the Authors

Amanda O. Latz, Ed.D., is an Assistant Professor of Adult, Higher, and Community Education in the Department of Educational Studies at Ball State University, where she teaches a variety of graduate-level courses. She holds a bachelor's degree in sociology with a minor in human resource development from James Madison University (2001), a master's degree in higher education administration from Appalachian State University (2006), and an Ed.D. in adult, higher, and community education (2011) as well as a Certificate in College and University Teaching (2009) from Ball State University. Her dissertation, titled *Understanding the Educational Lives of Community College Students Through Photovoice,* was funded in part by the Myra Sadker Doctoral Dissertation Award. Her research interests reside in the following areas: the lived experiences of individuals involved within the community college setting, particularly students and faculty; qualitative research methods; the scholarship of teaching and learning, especially innovative pedagogies; college and university faculty development; collegiate athletics; gender, social class, popular culture, and education; and gifted education. She has presented her research and theoretical papers at a number of national and international conferences. In addition, her work has appeared in a variety of peer-reviewed journals such as *Transformative Dialogues: Teaching and Learning Journal, Journal for the Study of Sports & Athletes in Education, Journal for the Education of the Gifted,* and *Academic Exchange Quarterly.*

Cheryll M. Adams, Ph.D., is the Director Emerita of the Center for Gifted Studies and Talent Development at Ball State University. She teaches online graduate courses in gifted education and elementary education. For the past 30 years she has served in the field of gifted education as a teacher of gifted students at all grade levels; Director of Academic Life at the Indiana Academy for Science, Mathematics, and Humanities; and as the principal teacher in the Ball State Institute for the Gifted in Mathematics program. Additionally, she has been the founder and director of various other programs for gifted students. Dr.

Adams has authored or coauthored numerous publications in professional journals, as well as several book chapters. She serves on the editorial review board for *Roeper Review, Gifted Child Quarterly, Journal for the Education of the Gifted,* and *Journal of Advanced Academics.* She has served on the Board of Directors of the National Association for Gifted Children (NAGC), has been president of the Indiana Association for the Gifted, and currently serves on the board of The Association for the Gifted, Council for Exceptional Children and the Florida Association for the Gifted. In 2002, she received the NAGC Early Leader Award.